Luhmann / Maturana / Namiki / Redder / Varela
Beobachter

Materialität der Zeichen

Herausgegeben vom Graduiertenkolleg Siegen

Reihe A, Band 3

Bandredaktion: Karin Obermeier, Volker Redder

Niklas Luhmann / Humberto Maturana /
Mikio Namiki / Volker Redder /
Francisco Varela

Beobachter

Konvergenz der Erkenntnistheorien?

Wilhelm Fink Verlag München

Die Deutsche Bibliothek – CIP-Einheitsaufnahme

Beobachter: Konvergenz der Erkenntnistheorien? / Niklas
Luhmann ... – 2. Aufl. – München: Fink, 1992
  (Materialität der Zeichen: Reihe A; Bd. 3)
  ISBN 3-7705-2829-8
NE: Luhmann, Niklas; Materialität der Zeichen / A

2. Auflage 1992

ISBN 3-7705-2829-8
© 1990 Wilhelm Fink Verlag München
Herstellung: Ferdinand Schöningh GmbH, Paderborn

Inhalt

Volker Redder
Ich sehe was, was Du nicht siehst 7

Francisco Varela
*On the Conceptual Skeleton of Current
Cognitive Science*.. 13

Mikio Namiki
*Some Controversies in the Epistemology
of Modern Physics* 25

Humberto Maturana
*The Biological Foundations of Self Consciousness
and the Physical Domain of Existence* 47

Niklas Luhmann
Sthenographie..119

Hinweise zu den Autoren 139

Volker Redder

Ich sehe was, was Du nicht siehst.

Der Beobachter als externer Beobachter, der in der Lage ist, falsch oder richtig zu beobachten, hat bekanntlich eine lange Tradition. Lag der europäischen Kultur seit der frühen Neuzeit die "klare" Unterscheidung zwischen dem Menschen als Subjekt der Beobachtung und der Welt als Objekt seiner Beobachtungen zugrunde, so führte zu Beginn des 19. Jahrhunderts die Einbeziehung des Menschen selbst in die Gegenstände seiner Beobachtung zu den bekannten erkenntnistheoretischen Problemen.

Heute beobachten wir uns beim Beobachten unserer selbst als Beobachter. Und die Eindeutigkeit der Grenze zwischen Beobachter und Beobachtungsgegenstand verschwindet zusehends zugunsten einer Vielfalt kontingenter Grenzziehungen.[2]

Dennoch scheint sich generell die Beobachtungstradition im Sinne der klassischen Subjekt/Objekt-Dichotomie ungehindert fortzusetzen. Zwar wird die Labilität menschlicher Wirklichkeitsbeziehungen akzeptiert und zumindest im Alltag mit einer Pluralität von Welten umgegangen, aber die Erwartung an die Wissenschaft - insbesondere an die Naturwissenschaften und die ihr anhängenden Technologien -, die *eine* objektive Wirklichkeit aufzudecken, bleibt unvermindert bestehen. Trotz der genannten intellektuellen Rahmenbedingungen einer im Sinne J.-F. Lyotards etikettierbaren "condition postmoderne" läßt sich nach den Aussagen des Soziologen N. Luhmann eine theoretische Aufarbeitung dieser Erkenntnisproblematik für die Philosophie und die Soziologie nicht erkennen.[3] Man verharrt im fundamentalistischen Reservat der richtigen Position und pflegt die Illusion, sich Wissen über die Wirklichkeit aneignen zu können.

Für die Physik und die Biologie lauten die Analysen der Bandautoren Mikio Namiki und Humberto Maturana ähnlich. Lediglich F. Varela konstatiert in seinen epistemologiegeschichtlichen Ausführungen einen Einfluß dieser Debatte auf neueste Entwicklungen in der Kognitions-, Immunologie- und Evolutionsforschung.

Eine zentrale Rolle bei der angemahnten theoretischen Aufarbeitung spielt der Beobachterbegriff. An einem Punkt des "Wankens" traditioneller europäischer Denkweisen und des Versagens gewohnter Beschreibungsmittel kann eine Focussierung auf den Beobachter zur Ausleuchtung der Erkenntniskapazitäten einzelner Wissenschaften und zur Entwicklung funktionaler Konzepte und Beobachtungsinstrumente beitragen. Denn "ob ich beobachte, Beobachtungen beobachte oder Beobachtungen von Beobachtungen, ist hinsichtlich der empirischen 'Härte' und hinsichtlich der diskursiven Anschlußmöglichkeiten höchst relevant."[4]

Die enge Verflechtung von Beobachter und Beobachtungsgegenstand, sowie die damit verbundene Unmöglichkeit objektiver Erkenntnis markieren den gemeinsamen Ausgangspunkt der vier Autoren dieses Bandes.

Während der Biologe F. Varela und der Physiker M. Namiki dazu eine Art epistemologiegeschichtliche Verlaufsskizze der Kognitionsforschung und der Physik vorstellen, zielen die Überlegungen H. Maturanas in Richtung einer grundlegenden Beschreibung der biologischen Konstitution des Beobachtens und damit der Erkenntnis. N. Luhmanns Überlegungen zu dem beim Beobachten notwendig auftretenden Problem der Paradoxie versuchen darüber hinaus, Lösungsvorschläge für den Umgang mit der diagnostizierten Beobachtungs- bzw. Erkenntnisproblematik zu liefern.

Im Einzelnen lassen sich die Schwerpunkte der vier Beiträge wie folgt umreißen:

Francisco Varela versucht für die Kognitionsforschung und die mit ähnlichen Problemen befaßten Bereiche der Evolutions- und Immunologieforschung grundlegende, die Innen/Außen-Dichotomie betreffende Entwicklungstendenzen zu skizzieren und ihre philosophischen Grundlagen offenzulegen. Er bezieht sich dabei insbesondere auf das Verblassen interaktionistischer, an der Informationsverarbeitung orientierter Modelle, zugunsten einer Berücksichtigung der Autopoiese lebender Systeme und ihrer strukturellen Kopplung mit der Umgebung.

Der Beitrag Mikio Namikis ist durch eine ähnliche, epistemologiegeschichtlich orientierte Schwerpunktsetzung gekennzeichnet. In der Physik haben sich spätestens seit den Kontroversen um die Quantentheorie und Heisenbergs Wahrscheinlichkeitsfunktion enorme Veränderungen hinsichtlich der Wirklichkeitsvorstellung und der grundlegenden Begriffe der klassischen Physik - Raum, Zeit, Materie und Kausalität - vollzogen. Dennoch ist die moderne Physik heute nach den Beschreibungen des japanischen Physikers als eine "science of matter" zu charakterisieren. Namiki problematisiert dies, indem er anhand der Erörterung verschiedener physikalisch-wissenschaftlicher Kontroversen (Auseinandersetzungen um die Quantenmechanik und Heisenbergs berühmte Unschärferelation, Einstein/Bohr-Debatte, "Schrödinger's cat"- Paradox) und mittels einer Darstellung der Einflüsse philosophischer Strömungen auf den Physiker und sein Forschungsprojekt, den Beobachter und die damit verbundene Debatte um die Frage einer unabhängig vom Beobachter existierenden physikalischen Realität in den Mittelpunkt seiner Betrachtungen stellt.

Eine grundlegende biologische Behandlung des Themas präsentiert der Biologe und Neurokybernetiker Humberto R. Maturana. Im Rahmen seiner Überlegungen zur Funktionsweise lebender Systeme betrachtet er Erkenntnis als ein biologisches Phänomen, das innerhalb der funktionalen Kohärenz der gesamten Biosphäre stattfindet. Von dieser 'strukturellen Kopplung' einer Einheit mit ihrem Medium ist der Beobachter nicht auszuschließen. Dies gibt der Wissenschaft ihre biologische Grundlage und macht sie zu einem von der Biologie des Beobachters abhängigen Bereich des Erkennens, in dem so etwas wie 'Objektivität' grundsätzlich in Klammern zu setzen ist.

Niklas Luhmann, der Maturanas Konzept der Autopoiese auf die Betrachtung sozialer Systeme angewandt und zu seiner Theorie selbstreferentieller Systeme weiterentwickelt hat, thematisiert den Beobachter entlang neuerer Diskussionen zur Paradoxieproblematik. Im Anschluß an die Logik George Spencer Browns, in der Erkennen als Beobachten und Beschreiben verstanden wird und Beobachten und Beschreiben als Unterscheiden und Bezeichnen, stellt er das Paradoxieproblem als ein notwendig mit dem Unterscheiden und dem Beobachten verbundenes Phänomen dar. "Jede Beobachtung braucht ihre Unterscheidung und also ihr Paradox der Identität des Differenten als ihren blinden Fleck, mit dessen Hilfe sie beobachten kann." In Abgrenzung gegen philosophiegeschichtlich ältere Bemühungen, Paradoxien als "Fehler im System" und als "Herausforderung an die Rationalität" zu eliminieren und in deutlicher Distanz zum "Paradoxien zelebrierenden, postmodernen Erstarrungstanz", versucht Luhmann aus der Perspektive einer "Kybernetik zweiter Ordnung" Ansätze eines deblockierenden und kreativen Umgangs mit Paradoxien zu liefern.

Aber wie steht es angesichts offensichtlicher gesellschaftlicher Risiken und Gefahren und der "diagnostizierten" Verflechtung von Beobachter und Beobachtungsgegenstand mit der notwendigen Leistungsfähigkeit von Beobachtern und Beobachtungsinstrumenten?

Vielleicht läßt sich das Problem im Sinne Luhmanns auf eine Mehrheit von vernetzten Beobachtern verteilen, die jeweils das beobachten, was für den anderen unbeobachtbar ist, unterstützt und koordiniert von einem Theorie-Switchboard, welches die Folgelasten von gemachten und zu machenden Unterscheidungen taxiert und ausbalanciert.

Also bitte keinen gemeinsamen Nenner! Aber vielleicht sehen Sie das anders?

Wie fingen doch die Vorträge der Autoren dieses Bandes in Dubrovnik, bzw. am Siegener Graduiertenkolleg an: "I invite you for a moment to leave behind your commonly accepted certainties and to engage in other ways of seeing!"

Anmerkungen

[1] Diese Formel entstammt dem Aufsatz "Autonomie und Autopoiese" von Francisco J. Varela, erschienen in dem von S. J. Schmidt herausgegebenen Band *Der Diskurs des Radikalen Konstruktivismus*. Sie bezeichnet demnach einen circulus fructuosus, wobei "F" für jede Art von Prozeß, Interaktion oder Rearrangement und "ɸ" für eine Form der Beziehung zwischen solchen Prozessen, also für ihre Art der Interdependenz steht. Darüber hinaus stellt sie eine Form der Selbstreferentialität dar: "F" sagt etwas über sich selbst aus, nämlich daß "F= ɸ (F)" der Fall ist.

[2] Vgl. dazu Gumbrecht, H.U./Müller-Charles, U., "Umwelten/ Grenzen - Eine Aporie-Spiel-Retrospektive". In: Joschka Fischer, Hg., *Ökologie im Endspiel*. Paderborn, S. 69-75.

[3] Vgl. dazu Luhmann, N., 1987, *Archimedes und wir*, Berlin, S. 14-37.

[4] Gumbrecht, H.U., 1988, "Flache Diskurse". In: Gumbrecht, H.U./Pfeiffer, K.L., Hgg., *Materialität der Kommunikation*. Frankfurt, S. 920.

Francisco J. Varela

On the Conceptual Skeleton of Current Cognitive Science

1. Introduction

I am a biologist who has been interested in the biological roots of cognitive phenomena. Thus, my perspective will be based on the scientific disciplines concerned with the study of the mind, that is the *cognitive sciences* today. These disciplines are naturally close to and interweaved with human experience, since they include and implicate the human mind. The basic argument I want to develop is this: in their current frontier, the cognitive sciences discover that knowledge cannot be explained as a mirror of nature, but rather that the knower and the known are co-implicated. This is, epistemologically, a theme dear to post-modern philosophy: the absence of a reference point, or *a lack of foundations*. This is in direct contradiction to the classical scientific tradition of objectivism, which physics has exemplified, until recently.

2. A Brief Cartography for the Cognitive Sciences

Having thus broadly outlined the direction of my presentation, let me start by going through the logic of research in the main lines of cognitive science today.

2.1 The basic cognitive "equation"

When we talk about cognition today we are faced with an issue that appears simultaneously and in parallel and mutually illuminating ways in three main areas at least. First, there are the brain sciences - everybody knows that cognition has something to do with talking heads. But, cognition is also central to immunology. That is the system which we normally consider as the defense system of the body, but which, in fact, is a defense system no more than the brain is a defense system. The immune system is in its own right a cognitive system. Finally, there is evolution, where the cognitive processes along the life of one individual which happen at the brain or at the immune system, can also appear and be discussed at the level of the scale of trans-individual change in phylogeny or evolution. These three areas seem to reflect each other back and forth. We won't have time, of course, to go into the details of the three lines of work, but I will be drawing lessons and examples from all three of these.

Let me now try to articulate for you four different views of what cognition is as it appears in these three areas. I am going to call these four points of views or theoretical frameworks: I, IIa, IIb and III for reasons that will be clear to you in what follows.

Cognition as a scientific activity didn't really start with what the historian of science would call a research program until after the war. It was known at the time as cybernetics (or more specifically the first order cybernetics). This is the tradition of J. von Neumann, N. Wiener, H. von Forster, among others. These pioneers considered cognition to be a relatively simple problem. It was couched in the most standard way which in fact we still use today: cognition appears as an articulation of something that is happening on an inside and an outside, in some kind of a rough equation:

$$\text{Cognitive science} = \text{knower} + \text{world}.$$

The creators of what we today consider cognitive science immediately fell into what was considered to be the obvious philosophical background of separating an inside and an outside, and cognition was a matter of seeing how that inside dealt with that outside.

2.2 Computationalism

By the time we come to 1956, this vague intuition has become fully formulated into a research program. Out of the very diffuse cloud that was the first sort of cybernetics of the 40's and the 50's came people like M. Minsky, J. McCarthy, or N. Chomsky. The core of this research program has to do with two main things: symbols and how to process those symbols. Cognition becomes a clearly defined process, where the inside becomes rules (or programs), and the outside becomes the information which is coded through the symbols, so that the relationship outside/inside becomes that of the acquisition or the circulation of information. This is what we may call the computational, symbolic, or cognitivist approach. To render it in an equational form:

I . Computationalism

cognition ≈ computation
rules for processing symbols ← environmental information

The basic idea, familiar to all, is that cognition is information processing. The common-sense is that there is information out there, which you can pick up, encode into symbols, and you can process those symbols and do something with them. If you are a brain, the information has to do with features of the world. This is, for instance, the case in the classic work on the visual cortex describing specific neurons in specific cortical areas that respond only to a little edge, in such and such a position and orientation. These are called "feature detectors," which would correspond to symbols in the brain; and the question arises, what would be the appropriate processing rules to produce adequate behavior. The same thing happened in immunology. The information is contained in the outside molecules, if you want to defend yourselves from bacterias and pathogens. You need appropriate symbols that are the antibody molecules, which are produced by lymphocytes. Those symbols actually encode that information; and the questions deal with the rules by which your system produces an appropriate defense. In evolution, the information takes the form of selective pressures from the environment. They get codified in the genes, and the rules are the way in which differential reproduction works, so that the fittest genes augment in a population.

To be sure, neither in immunology nor in evolutionary biology would people talk about a computational approach. In evolution, one would talk about the Darwinian synthesis or in immunology, about instructionist theories. However, my point is precisely to try and get to their common conceptual and epistemological backbone.

2.3 Emergence$_a$

Back in the 1970's there are some important conceptual crises in these areas. Crises that have not become fully clear until rather recently. The crises in the three fields are absolutely parallel and centered around the same issue: for computationalism the "inside" is a rather passive container. It contains symbols and rules. But it is fundamentally driven by this outside, by information.

This approach has severe limitations, and it breaks down, not just conceptually but empirically, quite rapidly. It became gradually more important to realize that this inside itself has a very rich structure. Therefore, the focus started to be, not on rules and symbols, but on the self-organizing capacities of this inside. By self-organizing capacities we mean, that whenever you look at either brains or the immune systems of evolution, what is "inside" is not an array of symbols manipulated by rules, but very active components that interact with each other in an highly cooperative, network-like fashion.

In immunology the idea landed like a bomb in 1974 when Nils Jerne observed that antibodies mostly bind to other antibodies and he proposed that the immune system is a true network. Similarly, in evolution people started to realize from various observations that it is absolutely silly to say that an organism is a set of traits or characteristics each one of which is determined by a gene, because what a gene does primarily is to influence other genes. The genome, the structure of the whole organism, is also a full network. One can rarely modify one gene without in fact modifying the entire phenotype. One can rarely tamper with the concentration of one antibody without moving the entire state of the immune system.

This is, needless to say, almost trivially true in the brain. One could hardly do something to a neuron without in fact affecting the entire neural system. For instance, let us go back to the famous edge detector that I mentioned before. People have repeated that classical observation for edge detectors over and over again. However, what was usually not emphasized in describing that experiment is that it only works if the animal is fully immobilized, anesthetized, and with all other senses blocked. In other words, only when you have reduced the environment and the life of the cat to just about nothing. The moment you allow the animal to start to move or to allow it other sensory modalities, then immediately the neuron that used to respond to a particular thing won't do so any more. It becomes highly contextual.

Today we tend to accept as relatively obvious that there is such a thing as self-organizing capacities, and there are plenty of examples and discussions of self-organizing mechanisms. But those ideas were considered quite suspect up until the 1970's. When Heinz von Forster introduced me to the notion of self-organization in1967/68, and I would try and talk to other people about this, they would say: "Don't bother with that stuff, it won't lead you anywhere." The mood has changed radically. Today we have the fashionable movement of connectionism in America. In brief: the main point in the transition from I to IIa consists of replacing an inside which is very parsimonious, to one which is rich and *surabundant*.

Thus, in the development of the brain, the question is not one of establishing the symbols and the rules, but rather how to get rid of an enormous amount of connectivity that is present in the fetus. That is, growing up is more a matter of getting simpler rather than of acquiring more complexity. The same thing holds in immunology: the basic idea of the so-called Clonal Selection Theories was to see the system as having an enormous diversity, which was then selected by the encounters with the antigen (foreign molecules) of the environment. This establishes the nature of the "inside."

What is the nature of the coupling with the environment? Well, in most of the current connectionist work, it consists of all the good information of the environment being picked up, albeit in a different form of representation. For example, the famous connectionist system NEtTalk can read pages of texts such as children's stories, and after a training phase, can learn to read any children's story in understandable English. The role of environmental information is still dominant. Thus, in its equational form we can say that:

IIa. Emergence$_a$: Connectionism

| cognition ≈ attractors |
| rich network self-organization ← environmental information |

2.4 Emergence$_b$

The transition from emergence$_a$ to emergence$_b$ has to do, not with the way the inside is understood, but with the outside. Instead of just carrying over the old notion of information pick-up, the outside is re-conceptualized as a selection of all the richness that can exist in the network. In this way, we are not dealing with information encoded in symbols, but rather with selection factors. Let us use a metaphor to explain the difference between I and IIb. In I, if you want to buy yourself a suit, you go to the tailor, he takes your measurements and cuts it for you. In the second sense of emergence IIb, you assume that there are department stores in the city and what you do is pick up the one that suits you best.

This is typically a selectionist point of view. It is also the old Darwinian notion of the survival of the fittest. In fact, people would say that it was Darwinian thought that allowed us to have a fresh look at what was happening in immunology and in the brain. G. Edelman, for example, proposes that the best theory of the brain is the selective theory in the sense of the Darwinian selection of self-organizing networks of neuronal populations. In immunology, the antigens or bacteria are supposed to select the antibodies that one keeps while growing up. This is known as the Clonal Selection Theory in Immunology. The difference between one individual and the other is precisely that each one of us will have been optimally selected by that antigenic molecular environment, trimming this rich internal immune network.

What is interesting in moving between the two senses of emergence, from an instructionist point of view to a selectionist one, is that the little arrow from the outside to the inside begins to change. Optimal selection is not just an encoding problem. The omni-presence of the environment, whatever that is, becomes somewhat weakened under the notion of a selection. It is not something directly encoded, it is only contingently and indirectly affecting, guiding, sculpting. So, equationally we can now write the previous arrow in dotted lines:

IIb. Emergence$_b$: Selectionism

cognition ≈ evolution
rich network self-organization ←--- selective optimization

2.5. Enaction

We said that for emergence$_b$, the metaphor is one of John going around to the department stores and finding the one suit which is best for him, a selective process. But in fact, what we can now notice is that John cannot buy a suit independently of the rest of the events in the society in which he exists: getting married, having kids, driving his car, and so on. In other words, if you study networks in the brain, i.e. if you just concentrate on the way the spinal cord and the motor cortex operate so that we can take a step, this clearly seems to be associated with a subpart, with a sub-network of the brain. If you look at it in isolation, it works very much as if it were an optimal machine, well adapted to that task. However, it is but one sub-network of a large assembly of other sub-networks in a highly interactive dialogue. When I move I also see, smell, and talk. All of these networks function somehow together, sub-networks that collaborate in a hyper-network. Thus, none of them can be considered to be doing something optimally because it is a large complex assembly. Similarly, it came as a shock to evolutionary biologists that the good old notion of Darwinian fitness is not well suited to account for what happens in evolution. The extent to which optimality may be a useful explanatory paradigm has just recently become a hot debate within evolutionary biology.

Here we need to introduce, then, another key notion: that of *modular* self-organizing networks. By modular, I mean that one cannot work with something that is a global strategy for cognition. In the 1950's people tried to build into artificial intelligence a General Problem Solver, a program abstract enough and powerful enough to solve any problem. Years later, researchers are now convinced that no GPS can exist. You can work only with modular, partial sub-networks and partial tasks. But when you try to put these together, there is no way to guarantee that they will function at some optimal level. It is more in the nature of a *bricolage* of several independent sub-components.

Now you see, the outside has moved from being the absolute reference point (in a very realist sense of what gets represented), to an optimal selection, receding one step into the background, but you'll still have some kind of a reference point on the outside in the form of optimality. Now, if even optimality has to go, then the arrow from outside becomes completely problematic since there are no reference points left. Here I need to redraw my arrow as something else, because it is not just something going from outside to inside. So, this is the point where we need to talk about *structural coupling*. The reason for using that particular form of describing the classical inside/outside distinction is to take one step away from the presuppositions about the nature of this coupling, beyond information, instruction, selection, or optimality. The move usually consists of the abandoning of any hope for a simple optimality, and looking at the ways in which system and environment define each other. So, instead of John just going out and buying the suit, we realize that he has the car, the family, and his desires as part of the social system which produces the suits he needs to buy, a totally circular situation. In fact, we realize that the interesting story cannot be told by having John as a focus of attention.

At this point, we can introduce what is in fact a very simple possibility: what is happening in cognition is that this capacity of having a rich self-organization reveals or *brings forth regularities*. Provided that there is any form of structural coupling with any form of contingency, a rich network will establish regularities. It cannot *but* bring about regularities. Now, once the regularities are established, it's easy to describe them by saying that the system is recognizing and adapting. Once this huge array of modular structures are present, never mind *where* that is, it will articulate a set of regularities.

I want to use the word *enactive* to denote the transition from an emergence perspective which drops the notion that whatever it is that we describe as regular environment can be defined independently of the history of coupling. Hence, the equational form:

III. Enaction

cognition ≈ bringing forth rich network self-organization ⇅ viable trajectories

The double arrow has now replaced a one-way arrow, even a weak one. This "double-sense" traffic is to underline the fact that both things emerge in co-ordination, in reciprocity.

3. Conjunctive clauses

Let *A* be the statement (the assertion, the observation, the principle, the mechanism), that self-organization in biological networks is an intrinsic property. Let *B* be the statement (principle, observation, conclusion, empirical constraint), that such networks are modular and therefore there is no global optimization criteria. Let *C* be the statement, that regularities are co-emergent, i.e., they result from an history of coupling, and are an inevitable consequence of A+B.

We can now see our three moments in cognitive science developing as progressively inclusive classes, as follows:

Three key *independent* processes:

- A = profligacy of biological networks
- B = modularity and non-optimization of sub-networks
- C = mutual enfoldment of organism-environment

	A	B	C
I	-	-	-
II a	X	-	-
II b	X	X	-
III	X	X	X

So, it becomes a matter of conjoining conditions that are not in themselves logically conjoined. One could have A without B, for instance, as neural networks modellers often do. Or, you could have B without A, modularity without network self-organization, a move well-known to neurobiologists. Now, I believe, C is a different situation, for I cannot imagine a mechanism for C, the co-dependent arising of regularities, unless B and A are present. But there is no logical *a priori* reason to make C depend upon an A and B.

But empirically, it is clear that the moment one has A and B, then C drops like an apple. Thus, the moment you have an immune system which is both rich and modular, it inevitably and immediately specifies and is specified by those regularities. In immunology these two things are almost literally so: when an antibody binds to the so-called antigen, this is so because it is found bound. There is no way a molecular profile out-there can be said to be an antigene unless it is binding. There is a regularity that is inseparable from the antibody network. In this way, the molecular world in which you live is constantly brought forth.

It seems that the basic epistemological lesson of all this is: what we are left with once you get to III is a situation in which you can not rely on having *foundations*, an external reference point to serve as foundation. Whatever is regular, is a condition inseparable from your co-implicative history, it is not sitting out-there. Confronting that absence of foundation, is, for our traditional epistemologies, a rather tricky situation. But that's the challenge where biological research seems to be taking us.

Mikio Namiki

Some Controversies in the Epistemology of Modern Physics

Modern physics is a science of matter. Most physicists believe that nature has a sort of "matter hierarchy" composed of many strata or levels. Roughly speaking, modern physics is characterized by two kinds of research directions convergent with each other: the first, the search for constituents of matter at deeper levels; the second, consideration of how matter at a particular level is composed of deeper constituents. Physicists are sometimes influenced in their research work by their own philosophical or epistemological thinking, whether they are going to enter into an unknown level, or whether they want to understand strange behaviors of matter in a new world. For this reason serious controversies have occurred among physicists, not only about physical problems but also the philosophical or epistemological implications of physics. In the following I will survey some of these controversies.

1. Matter hierarchy and related problems

Let us consider a diagram of nature and modern physics (see following page). The vertical and horizontal directions show us the two kinds of research interests of modern physics, the former, the search for constituents of matter and the second, the analysis of structures of matter.

Let us first look at the diagram along the vertical direction. We know that familiar things, such as stones, tables, books, plants, animals, our bodies, etc., are composed of molecules and atoms, and furthermore that molecules and atoms are composed of nuclei and electrons. A nucleus is a composite particle of protons (p) and

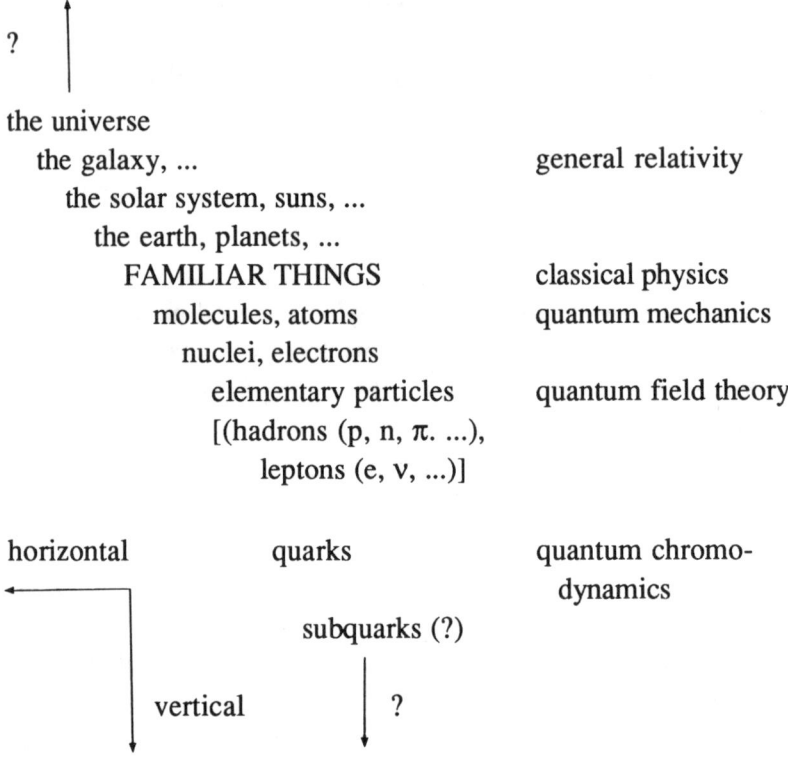

force originating mainly in the exchange of pions (π). A neutron decays into three particles, i.e., a proton, an electron (e) and a neutrino (ν). p, n and π are members of the "hadron" family of elementary particles, while e and ν belong to the "lepton" family. We have now reached the level of the elementary particle, at which the hadron and lepton families are located. At present, we have evidence that a hadron is made from a few "quarks" which are considered to be deeper constituents of matter. Some physicists suppose that "subquarks" should exist at the next level. I do not know what is at the bottom of matter. Research work which deals with this question, i.e. that heads downward in the vertical direction, has developed into what is called modern particle physics.

On the other hand, familiar things and similar materials make up the earth and other planets which are members of our solar system. Many suns compose our galaxy which belongs to the next higher level, and we know that the universe is composed of many galaxies. I do not know what kind of larger universe wraps the universe. Research work heading in this direction developed into what is called modern cosmology. Recent cosmology tells us that since the "big bang," the universe has been evolving from a very small primeval one to the present one, converging on every level of the "matter hierarchy." Consequently, we know that particle physics should be joined to cosmology in the research work of analyzing the "matter hierarchy."

Each level of the "matter hierarchy" is characterized by its own dynamics. Both familiar things and the solar system are subject to classical physics, its representative being Newtonian mechanics. Quantum mechanics governs the atomic and nuclear levels. Quantum field theory is responsible for elementary particles. Following standard particle physics, quarks are considered to be governed by quantum chromodynamics. On the other hand, cosmological evolutions of galaxies and/or the universe should be described by general relativity. Each dynamics has its own appearance or character different from the other. However, they are closely related to the others in the following way. Quantum mechanics becomes Newtonian mechanics in the case in which the Planck constant can be regarded as very small. Relativistic mechanics is also very close to the Newtonian mechanics when particle velocities are much smaller than the light velocity. We have reason to believe that all dynamics could be unified in a unique dynamic principle, with perfect symmetries inside the primeval universe immediately after the "big bang."

When we consider the horizontal direction of the diagram, we have to solve the problem of how matter at a particular level is made up of its constituents. For example, nuclear physics has been studying structures of nuclei in terms of nuclear constituents, i.e., protons and neutrons. Atomic physics has been analyzing electron configurations surrounding an atomic nucleus. Modern solid-state physics is engaged in the research work of knowing the structures of semi-conductors, macro-molecules and so on, in terms of constituents, i.e., crystal-lattices and electrons, or atoms and molecules. We know that solid-state physics is one of the sound bases of electronics and other material sciences upon which modern technologies have been developed. Modern physics also produced biophysics along one branch of the horizontal direction.

Extrapolating the trend, one may imagine that future physicists will perhaps want to create a science dealing with economics, politics, sociology, etc. Here we can recognize the existence of a sort of "matter(?) hierarchy" composed of organic cells, living individuals, communities or societies, nations and the international world. A famous Japanese critic named such an aggressive trend of modern physics, "physics imperialism." In fact, modern physics has already invaded the territory of chemistry and biology in this century. The science of matter was the subject of chemistry over one hundred years ago. In any case, it is important to consider modern physics from both points of view: from fundamental dynamics and the model-making of deeper constituents.

In this context I have to talk about the introduction of neutrino by W. Pauli in 1932 and the proposal of the meson theory by H. Yukawa in 1935. Many new experimental facts discovered in the "miracle" year 1932 were strange phenomena, as if they could not be understood within the framework of existing dynamic principles. Most physicists wanted to break through those difficult problems again by changing the dynamic principles. Such a revolutionary trend is understandable if we take into account that physicists were at that time working in a context only ten years after the construction of quantum mechanics. However, the neutrino hypothesis solved the problem by keeping the conservation law of energy, and the meson theory succeeded in deriving nuclear force within the framework of quantum field theory. Both were not a matter of fundamental dynamics but of new substantial elements. Nevertheless, this introduction of new elements was not accepted for a rather long time. N. Bohr did not have any interest in Yukawa's theory when he first heard the proposal during his stay in Japan. Even after recognizing their successes, the trend to reject the inclusion of new hypothetical substances or constituents was prevalent in many physicists' thinking for a very long time.

In the following, I want to describe a controversy which happened over twenty years ago in the search for a possible level of matter beyond the elementary particle. The American physicist G. Chew wanted to stop the "class strife" among microscopic particles (i.e., the "matter hierarchy"), considering the bottom of matter to be at the level of the elementary particle. According to his idea, elementary particles are composed of elementary particles themselves. He attempted to concretely formulate his theory by means of the so-called "bootstrap" mechanism. To be interesting, he named his idea "nuclear democracy" after American democracy.

Contrary to Chew's idea, W. Heisenberg and H. Yukawa were willing to find the bottom of matter at the level one-step deeper than that of the elementary particle. They considered an elementary particle to be a particular mode of oscillation of a hypothetical "Urmaterie" (Heisenberg) or of a possible "elementary region" of the space-time domain (Yukawa). Indeed, they wanted to solve every problem in particle physics by means of their theories. Someone once said jokingly that they intended to finish off physics before their retirement. Unfortunately, they were not able to obtain very many followers.

A quite different idea on "matter hierarchy" was proposed by the Japanese physicist S. Sakata. He supposed the "matter hierarchy" to be endless. Extending a preliminary idea given by E. Fermi and C.N. Yang, he proposed a "composite model" of hadrons in which a hadron was considered to be composed of three kinds of more fundamental particles. Improving Sakata's model, the American physicist M. Gell-Mann presented the quark model which resulted in the standard theory of present particle physics. Sakata further proposed a proto-type of the subquark model for the purpose of unifying hadrons and leptons at a deeper level.

The controversy happened mainly between the schools of the nuclear democracy and the composite models, evoking philosophical and scientific discussions with political implications. At least in

Japan, those who wanted to develop the nuclear democracy were regarded as conservatives, while those belonging to the school of the composite model behaved as if they were reformists. One may recall the historical opposition between the "Energetik" and the "Atomistik" in Europe one hundred years ago. The research of a physicist often reflects his philosophical or ideological position. We can also observe other remarkable examples of serious oppositions among outstanding physicists for the epistemological implications of quantum mechanics, as will be discussed later.

In this context, it is interesting to talk about Mao Tse-Tung's interest in particle physics. Over twenty years ago he read Sakata's paper that appeared in a Japanese journal of physics, in which Sakata described the above idea of the endless "matter hierarchy" in a dialogic form. Mao was attracted to Sakata's idea because of his philosophical point of view and wrote a paper on physics in a journal of the Chinese Communist Party. According to Mao, the revolution will be repeated endlessly, because new conflicts will inevitably be produced in a new society born after each revolution. I think, it was natural that Mao admired Sakata's idea. He recommended Chinese physicists to construct their particle physics along this Maoist perspective. In my first visit to China immediately after the beginning of the so-called "Cultural Revolution" in 1966, I met many Chinese physicists who were armed with such Maoist thought. They proposed the "straton" model to analyze the hadron structure. It was a modeling of the idea of the endless "matter hierarchy."

It is obvious that particle physics has been developing for the past twenty years along the line of thought rooted in the composite instead of in the nuclear democracy model. It seems that Chew's idea could not survive in standard particle physics. Most physicists now believe in the existence of the "quarks" even though they have not yet been found as ordinary particles. However, no one knows whether "matter hierarchy" is endless or not. If we literally accept the idea of the endless "matter hierarchy," we have to read an endless reductionism or a sort of agnosticism in the idea. Furthermore, I have a naive question as to whether the idea of the endless "matter hierarchy" is consistent with the story of evolution of the universe, because the universe should meet with infinitely many levels of matter for a finite time from the "big bang" onwards. The next problem of particle physics is to substantially ascertain what are the quarks and to find the dynamics governing them. These dynamics are also expected to have a close connection with cosmological problems.

Modern physics is now aiming at a total understanding of nature, from the bottom to the top of the "matter hierarchy" and from possible microscopic constituents to the human being.

2. *Elements of quantum mechanics*

Quantum mechanics is built on the experimental basis of the *wave-particle* duality, which is one of the most important characters of microscopic particles. Before quantum mechanics, we considered light to be a (classical) wave but the electron to be a (classical) particle. Now we know that both light and the electron have wave-particle duality, or roughly speaking, they should be regarded as a *wave-or-particle*. However, the wave-or-particle is neither a classical wave nor a classical particle, as will be seen below. The *wave* nature of the wave-or-particle is experimentally recognized only through the interference or diffraction phenomena, while its *particle* nature only means that a particle cannot be divided. We ought not imagine any other classical natures beyond these.

First of all, quantum mechanics tell us that a particle with a definite momentum, say p, and a definite energy, say E, is described by a wave with a definite wave-length, $\lambda = h/p$, and a definite frequency, $\nu = E/h$, h being the Planck constant. Starting from this fact, we can derive the famous Heisenberg uncertainty principle, $\Delta x \Delta p \sim h$ and $\Delta t \Delta E \sim h$, in which Δx, Δp, Δt and ΔE are, respectively, uncertainties of position, momentum, time and energy. Briefly, the uncertainty principle states that we cannot simultaneously measure position and momentum or time and energy with an arbitrary accuracy. Needless to say, this is one of the most important characters of quantum mechanics, different from classical mechanics, which is closely related to the quantum measurement problem.

Generally, a state of motion of a quantum mechanical particle is represented by a wave function, say $\Psi(x,t)$, x and t denoting a space-time point, respectively. The basic postulates of quantum mechanics, to be imposed on the wave function, consist of a) the superposition principle; b) the probability interpretation; c) the Schrödinger equation. The superposition principle states that if two kinds of motion, say a and b, which are described by wave functions Ψ_a and Ψ_b, respectively, are possible in a dynamic system, we should represent its state with a wave function given by $\Psi=\Psi_a+\Psi_b$. The probability interpretation is that $P(x,t)=|\Psi(x,t)|^2$ should give the probability of finding the particle at x and t in a state described by Ψ. These postulates are set up on the experimental basis of the wave-particle duality.

I will try to explain the wave-particle duality through a simple Young-type interference experiment. See Fig. 1, which illustrates the experiment that an incident beam of particles with momentum, p, (i.e., a wave with wave-length, $\lambda=h/p$) coming up from the bottom makes a beautiful interference pattern on the screen, after passing through two small slits, a and b. This is nothing other than the experimental evidence of the *wave* nature. The form of the interference pattern is determined by wave-length and distances between a and b and between the slits and the screen. Denoting two partial waves after passing through a and b by wave functions Ψ_a and Ψ_b respectively, we have $\Psi=\Psi_a+\Psi_b$ in the upper side of the slits, according to the superposition principle. The probability interpretation teaches us that the particle distribution on the screen is proportional to

$$P=|\Psi_a+\Psi_b|^2=P_a+P_b+2\mathrm{Re}(\Psi_a\Psi_b^*) \qquad \text{Eq. (1)}$$

where Ψ_b^* is the complex conjugate of Ψ_b, $P_a=|\Psi_a|^2$ and $P_b=|\Psi_b|^2$. Equation (1) tells us that P is not a simple sum of P_a and P_b due to the presence of the interference term, $2\mathrm{Re}(\Psi_a\Psi_b^*)$. This is the common mathematical mechanism of interference phenomena to show the wave nature. Remember that the superposition principle for wave functions never gives a simple sum of probabilities.

If the wave were classical, we could observe the same (but very weak) pattern even for an extremely weak beam. However, the interference pattern is no longer kept for an extremely weak beam of quantum-mechanical particles. Suppose an ideal experiment in which we send one particle to the slits by every one second and then detect one particle on the screen by every on second. Experimentally, we have only a one-spot distribution on the screen around a point, say Q, at which we detected the particle, so that the interference pattern itself is completely lost. This is the experimental evidence of the *particle* nature that a particle cannot be divided. Nevertheless, each particle retains the wave nature, because the original interference pattern can be reproduced again by accumulating many independent spots. This is the experimental behavior of the *wave-particle* duality.

In the above ideal experiment, we cannot find the particle at any other place than Q immediately after the detection, so that the experiment causes the following change of the wave function:

$$\Psi \rightarrow \Psi_Q \qquad \text{Eq. (2)}$$

where Ψ_Q distributes only around Q. The change is called "wave packet reduction" or "wave function collapse" by measurement (by the position measurement in this case), which is a logical consequence of the probability interpretation. However, the "wave packet reduction" is an acausal and probabilistic event but not a causal process to be described by the Schrödinger equation itself, becuse we cannot know, before the measurement, where we shall find the particle for the same initial state Ψ. Consequently, a question arises as to whether the measurement process can be described by quantum mechanics itself. This is the starting point of the quantum measurement problem.

Let us return back to the above interference experiment. If we detect the particle at one slit a (or b) by an appropriate detector, then we have no probability of finding it at another slit b (or a) because of the particle nature and the probability interpretation. In other words, Ψ_b (or Ψ_a) disappears by the detection. This means that such a "wave packet reduction" as

$$\Psi \rightarrow \Psi_a \text{ (or } \Psi \rightarrow \Psi_b) \qquad \text{Eq. (3)}$$

takes place by the determination of the particle path. Therefore, we must have the particle distribution proportional to only P_a (or only P_b) on the screen. The resultant accumulated distribution, corresponding to the determination of the particle path a or b, is naturally proportional to a simple sum P_a and P_b without the interference term in Eq. (1). Consequently, we can conclude that the measurement leading us to the determination of the particle path completely destroys the interference pattern. In this case, the "wave packet reduction" by measurement is to be represented by the disappearance of the interference term, i.e., by the process

$$P \rightarrow P_a + P_b \qquad \text{Eq. (4)}$$

Compare this with Eq. (1). The "wave packet reduction" by measurement is characterized by the simple sum of probabilities. Possible measurement theories have to analyze the mechanism of erasing the interference term.

In the above discussions, we have seen that a measurement on a quantum-mechanical system has generally destroyed its initial-state wave function. The fact, as well as the uncertainty principle, is a matter of principle, which is very far from classical common-knowledge familiar to us. In a classical system we can always find an experimental method, which enables us to measure a physical quantity without giving disturbances to the system.

Usually, most of quantum-mechanical measurements are decomposed in a set of many yes-no experiments. An yes-no experiment is so designed as to give the answer "yes" or "no" to a measurement proposition, say *A*. Supplementing the above interference experiment with appropriate equipment, we can make a definite correspondence of the particle path, a, to a proposition, A, and therefore, of the particle path, b, to *not A*. In this case, Eq. (4) describes the "wave packet reduction" by measurement of *A*.

Recently, J.A. Wheeler presented an interesting proposal named "delayed choice experiment" to examine the wave-particle duality (see Fig. 2). In the proposed experiment, a light pulse including only one photon is first divided by a half mirror, M_1, into two parts running two channels, I and II. The optical paths of I and II are so designed as to be much longer than the pulse lenght. In Case A the two partial waves are separately guided to two detectors, D_I and D_{II}. Quantum mechanics predicts that if D_I (or D_{II}) generates a signal of catching the photon, then D_{II} (or D_I) must give no signal because of the particle nature of the photon. In this case, we must observe the particle nature of the photon. On the other hand, in Case B, the two partial waves are gathered again in I and II, by another half mirror, M_2. Quantum mechanics predicts that we must observe the interference effects, by D_I and D_{II}, to show the wave nature of the photon. Wheeler proposed to choose Case A or Case B (i.e., with or without M_2) after each pulse passed through the first half mirror. C.O. Allay and H. Walther successfully performed their experiments to show that quantum mechanics gave correct predictions.

One of the interesting points of the "delayed choice experiment" ist that each photon does not know, which nature (wave or particle) it shows, until the observer decides to choose Case A or Case B. Therefore, Wheeler claims that there should exist no phenomena (or no actual past) before a recording or registration by the observer. His argument will necessarily evoke serious controversies on the epistemology of quantum mechanics.

On the other hand, it is also noticed that if the observer decides to choose one of both cases and afterword detects the photon by D_I (or D_{II}), he can immediately know the result of detection by another detector without explicit observation. Quantum mechanics behaves in this case as if there were a non-local long-distance correlation between observations by both detectors. We can also see the same kind of long-distance correlation in the cases of the "wave packet reduction" as mentioned above. Actually, if we detect a particle at a point, then we can immediately know that it does not exist at any other place. In other words, we can obtain the information as if it were instantly transmitted. Such a non-local long-distance correlation, which appears everywhere where a quantum-mechanical character stands out, plays an essential role in the famous Einstein-Podolsky-Rosen paradox, as will be seen in the next section.

3. Controversies on the quantum measurement problem

The quantum measurement problem is an analysis of the physical contents of quantum-mechanical measurement processes and to discuss their epistemological implications. Controversies on the problem are divided into two classes. Controversies of the first class happened between those who agree and disagree with the Copenhagen interpretation of quantum mechanics. The typical and the most famous controversy was that between A. Einstein and N. Bohr, on Einstein's question whether quantum mechanics can completely describe physical reality. Controversies of the second class are concerned with the problem, within the framework of the Copenhagen interpretation, whether the "wave packet reduction" can be described by quantum mechanics itself or not. The controversy between E. P. Wigner and L. Rosenfeld provides us here with an example.

3.1 The Einstein-Bohr Controversy and Related Problems

Einstein criticized quantum mechanics on the basis of his criterion of *physical reality*: Every element of a physical reality must have a counter part in physical theory. If, without in any way disturbing a system, we can predict with certainty (i.e., with probability equal to unity) the value of a physical quantity, then there exists an element of physical reality corresponding to this physical quantity. The criterion clearly came out of a classical point of view. Together with B. Podolsky and N. Rosen, Einstein presented a paradox, which was known as the Einstein-Podolsky-Rosen (EPR) paradox.

Let us briefly consider the EPR paradox. Consider a dynamic system composed of two particles, say I and II, with a definite correlation in such a way that, if I has a property a or b, II must have a property b or a, respectively. Suppose properties, a and b, are exclusive of each other, which are represented, for example, by two values of a dichotomous dynamic variable. Mathematically, its quantum-mechanical state is written as $\Psi = (\Psi_a^I \Psi_b^{II} + \Psi_b^I \Psi_a^{II})/\sqrt{2}$, according to the superposition principle. After II goes far away from I, we try to measure the property of I. In this case, quantum mechanics predicts that, when we find property a (or b), then we must immediately know that II has property b (or a), because the "wave packet reduction," $\Psi \to \Psi_a^I \Psi_b^I$ (or $\to \Psi_b^I \Psi_a^{II}$), takes place. The transmission velocity from II to I (or to us) is infinity! Here the non-local long-distance correlation, which we have already discussed, much more clearly stands out in the form of a two-particle correlation.

The measurement on I must never disturb II (because II is far from I), so that we have obtained information about II without disturbing II. According to the above criterion, we can consider the dynamic variable to be an element of physical reality. However, we must conclude that II definitely has property b (or a) from the outset. Through similar arguments on the measurement of another variable of I in the same initial state, we can draw another conclusion that II definitely has another property from the outset. Einstein considered it to be a contradiction to show the fact that quantum mechanics never describes any kind of physical reality existing independently of observers.

The EPR paradox holds under the assumption that measurements on I never disturb II located far from I. However, Bohr claimed that the very assumption did not hold, because a correlated system is not considered to be separable and hence, a measurement on I must necessarily act on the whole system including II. This character of quantum mechanics is called "non-separability," which is the origin of the non-local long-distance correlation mentioned above. Bohr believed that Einstein's physical reality existed only in the classical world but not in the quantum-mechancial one. The controversy was certainly based on a definite difference of their epistemological attitudes toward nature.

It is true that quantum mechanics is not compatible with Einstein's physical reality, but we can hardly understand the non-separability or the non-local long-distance correlation from our familiar point of view. For this reason, the EPR paradox evoked the fundamental questions and many controversies that have continued for these fifty years, as to whether *physical reality* exists independent of observers or not in the quantum-mechanical world, or as to whether the non-local long-distance correlation can actually be observed or not. Those who are eager to keep the "separability," as in classical physics, have been searching for a possible way of replacing quantum mechanics with a classical stochastic-dynamic theory. Up to the present, however, I do not think that they have been successful. All experiments (including A. Aspect's beautiful one) seem to strongly support quantum mechanics but not Einstein. No matter how some physicists consider the present theory to be unaceptable, quantum mechanics will continue to work as a central dynamics of the microscopic world, although it will be modified for new constituents or phenomena. I think that an important key to solving the problem of physical reality or non-separability will be found on a new horizon of frontier physics, and not in the present attempts of direct modification of quantum mechanics.

3.2 Wave packet reduction by measurement

The quantum measurement theory should theoretically derive the "wave packet reduction" by measurement by applying quantum mechanics to the total system composed of a microscopic object system, say Q, and a macroscopic apparatus system, say A. As was explained in the preceding section, we have to erase the interference term in Eq. (1), as a result of interaction between Q and A, in order to reach the "wave packet reduction" being represented by a simple sum of probabilities.

The first important theory of quantum measurements was formulated by J. von Neumann and developed by E.P. Wigner. Throughout their theory, they wanted to maintain the superposition principle as a very important principle by which the wave function is summable but the probability is not. Consequently, their theory never yielded the "wave packet reduction." Wigner continues in this mode claiming that the quantum measurement problem cannot be solved within the present theoretical framework of quantum mechanics. Von Neumann and Wigner considered the "Abstraktes Ich" or "consciousness" to give the "wave packet reduction" at the end of a chain of observations connecting the object to the observer. The theory also insists that the cut-point of the chain of observations (Q → Q → eyes of the observer → his nerve system → his brain cells → ...), to divide the observer-side from the object-side, can freely be moved, and that every measurement process at every cut-point can never give the "wave packet reduction" as long as it is a physical process.

It was natural that the introduction of the "Abstraktes Ich" or "consciousness" evoked many serious objections and controversies. E. Schrödinger presented the famous "Schrödinger's cat" paradox to criticize their theory. Let us briefly explain his paradox here. Suppose that we have two boxes. The first box contains a small amount of radioactive isotope and a detector, whereby we place a cat and a bottle of poisonous gas in the second box. The second box is equipment so designed as to destroy the bottle by an electric signal sent from the detector in the first box. If the radioactive isotope is kept in an excited state, the detector generates no signal and then the cat remains alive. If the radioactive isotope emits radiation by its decay to the ground state, the detector catches it and then generates an electric signal by which the cat is killed. The "alive" or "dead" cat indicates whether the radioactive isotope is, respectively, in the excited or ground state. However, the observer has to open the window of the box, in order to look at the cat, that is, in order to know the result of the measurement. According to the von Neumann theory, this looking-in is also a quantum-mechanical measurement on the chain of observations. Thus we have to conclude that the cat is in a superposed state of the "alive" and "dead" states before this looking-in accompanied by consciousness. In other words, only the looking-in can yield the "wave packet reduction" of the cat state to be "alive" or "dead". How strange! It would be natural to consider that the cat is surely alive or dead independent of the looking-in, and that the essential process of the quantum-mechanical measurement is already completed inside the detector.

One of the most important oppositions to the von Neumann-Wigner theory came from the ergodic amplification theory, which was proposed by many authors but representatively formulated by L. Rosenfeld and the Milan group (A. Daneri, A. Loinger and G.M. Prosperi). They consider the quantum measurement process in the following way: A microscopic object system is so small that it cannot have energy enough to drive a macroscopic apparatus system. Therefore, we have to supply energy through an amplification process, such as discharge phenomena in counters, which inevitably becomes a thermal irreversible process capable of erasing the interference term. They destroyed the superposition principle to get the "wave packet reduction," contrary to the von Neumann-Wigner theory. Thus both schools fell into a very serious controversy. They exchanged a few emphatic criticisms with each other through publications. When I was working at the Niels Bohr Institute, Copenhagen, about twenty years ago, I attended Rosenfeld's lecture entitled "Recent controversy in the epistemology of quantum mechanics." I clearly recall that he was extremely annoyed by Wigner.

Today Wigner still adheres to the introduction of "consciousness" from his philosophical point of view, while Rosenfeld has strictly rejected it and tried to obtain the "wave packet reduction" without resorting to such a metaphysical element. This controversy was also rooted in a definite difference of their epistemological attitudes towards nature. Wigner criticized the ergodic amplification theory through the following two points: a) Wigner's theorem, stating a mathematical fact almost equivalent to keeping of the superposition principle; b) the negative-result-measurement paradox, which shows that we can find a measurement process leading us to the "wave packet reduction" without resorting to any kind of thermal irreversible processes.

I agree with Wigner in the second point, so that I do not think that the ergodic amplification theory can solve the problem. However, I would never agree that the von Neumann-Wigner theory is correct. I have found a possible way of breaking through Wigner's theorem and could formulate my theory of quantum measurements leading us to the "wave packet reduction" without resorting to either "consciousness" or any kind of thermal irreversible processes. This is my position.

4. Final remarks

Finally, I would like to consider East-West relations in science from the standpoint of a Japanese. In ancient times Asia was one of the most important places of creating and supplying advanced sciences and technologies to the world. Nevertheless, Asia could not create modern science, while Europe did so beautifully. I think, it is a big mystery in the world that modern science was not born and not developed in India or China. Why it was born only in Europe is really an interesting question. I have no convincing answer to this question.

Of course, modern science is quite international and no distinction should exist between European and Asian sciences. However, I often experience some subtle differences between European and Japanese scientists. Let me use the example of my experiences in studying the quantum measurement theory. The problem is conspicuously philosophical. I was surprised by the fact that not a small number of physicists in Europe were earnestly engaged in such a very fundamental or rather philosphical problem. Most Japanese physicists are much more pragmatic. In fact, only a few persons in Japan are working in this area. Furthermore, I am very much impressed by the fact that some European physicists persist in rooting their physical theories in their own philosophical positions, as was seen in the preceding section, and that they also want to base their philosophical principles or spiritual lives based upon their own theories of physics. It is said that European people are thinking nature in a logical and analytical way, while Japanese people have been willing to quietly contemplate it, mainly based on their sensivity. I am wondering whether or not Japanese sensivity is suitable to scientific works. Another question may also arise as to whether such situations stem from the religious difference between Christian and Asian religions, because Christianity seems to us to be more dogmatic than Asian ones.

However, the Asian way of thinking could also be a possible basis to promote natural sciences. For example, we may observe in H. Yukawa's scientific life a remarkable style somewhat different from the European one. He was educated by the Chinese classics. He often referred to the writings of ancient Chinese philosophers in his research. His famous work, the meson theory, is a product of such thinking. His proposal was not accepted for a while in Europe, as was mentioned in the first section. It might have been a heretical consideration in Europe at that time. Of course, I cannot clearly differentiate the direct relationship between the meson theory and his way of thinking based on Chinese classics. In any case, however, I am interested in the humanities as a possible background of natural sciences at a deeper level.

Besides the meson theory, Yukawa had a great influence upon those around him, especially, upon S. Tomonaga and S.Sakata. It was well known that Tomonaga intended to formulate his famous quantum electrodynamics under Yukawa's suggestion. Sakata made his epistemological methodology of particle physics, including the endless "matter hierarchy," on the basis of Yukawa's idea of introducing the meson theory and the philosophy of materialism.

Yukawa, Tomonaga and Sakata were also interested in the measurement problem from their own philosophical points of view, even though unfortunately they left us few writings on the problem. Each of their own philosophical views ought to be considered in the measurement problem. N. Bohr once mentioned that European physicists could not accept quantum mechanics without some mental difficulties, while some Japanese physicists seemed to more easily receive it. He might be looking for the reason in cultural differences. I am not yet satisfied by my own thinking about this problem.

Here, I must mention two different attitudes towards sciences that I have observed among Japanese scientists. Some scientists want to cultivate their philosophical background through their scientific works, while others want to do science apart from their spiritual lives. Yukawa must be considered a representative of those holding the former attitude. As for the latter, we need to recall the prominent social position and meaning of modern science-technology in Japan.

Japan came in direct contact with European (and American) sciences and technologies after the Meiji revolution, in which my country changed its political and social system from the feudal one to the modern one after a three hundred year period of national isolation. About one hundred and thirty years ago an American fleet came to Japan and enforced the Japanese feudal government to open the country. Its attack on Japan was one of the very important pressures to promote the Meiji revolution. Big warships were a symbol of advanced Western countries having strong powers. The Meiji Government was eager to obtain such a strong power by means of Western sciences and technologies. The slogan to promote sciences and technologies was "Japanese Spirit and Western Techniques." Europeans could say that the Japanese were ignorant of the cultural background of Western science and technology closely related to European spiritual life. To most Japanese people, science was only a set of rules to make powerful arms or convenient tools or to analyze mysterious phenomena. Such a tendency still exists generally among the Japanese people, sometimes, even among scientists. It seems that Japanese science and technology has been taking a separate path from Japanese spiritual life. Along this line of development Japan has achieved industrial and economical successes. It might be true that Yukawa and a few pioneer scientists were previously exceptional examples in Japan, but they also indicated that Japanese culture allowed for some developments in modern science.

Finally, I would like to say that Asian cultures, including the Japanese one, had already been well cultivated or prepared for the modern sciences before their contact with Western sciences and technologies. I believe that Asian people have a great possibility of creating and developing a modern science rooted in their own cultures.

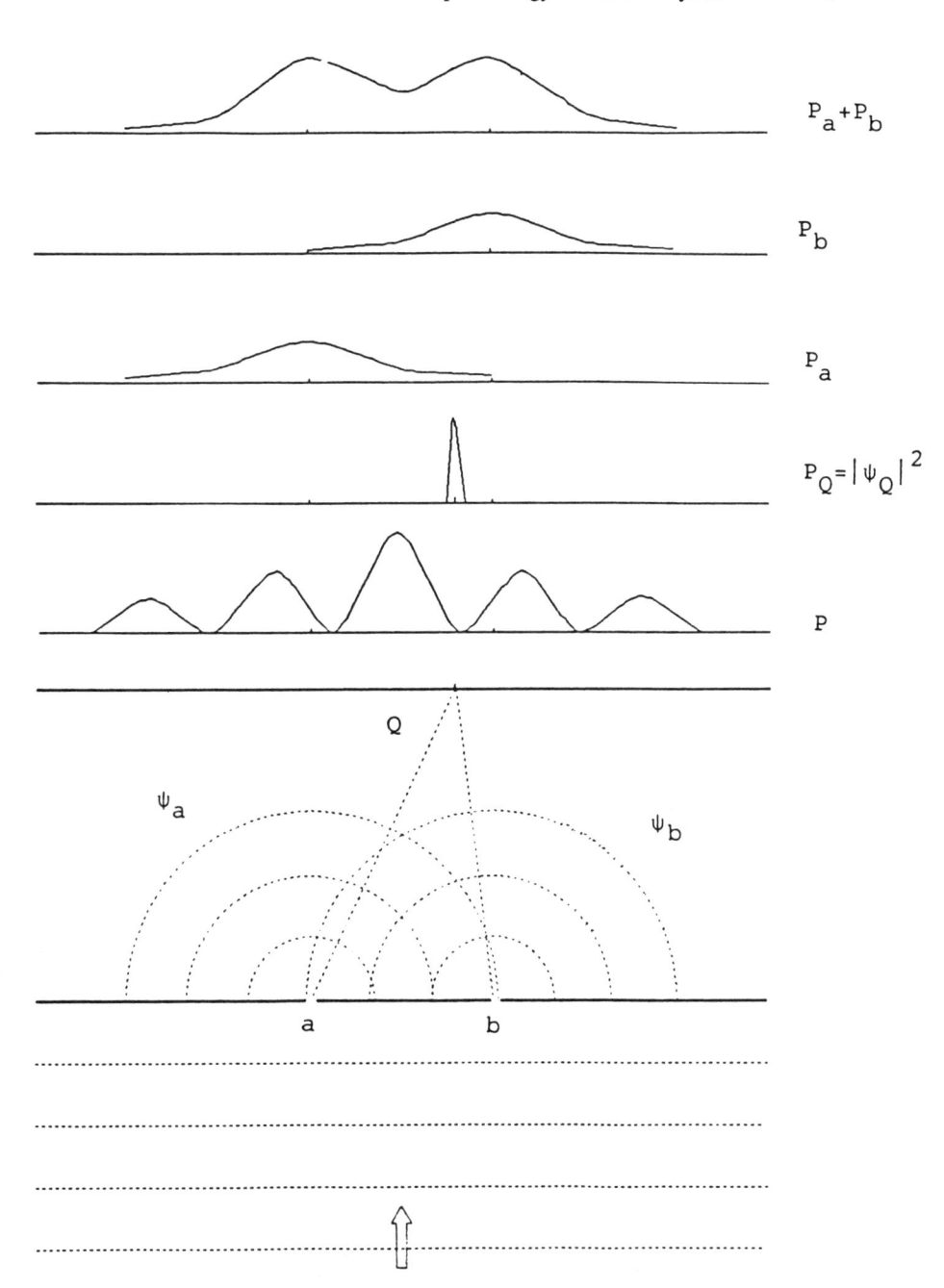

Fig. 1 Interference experiment

Case A

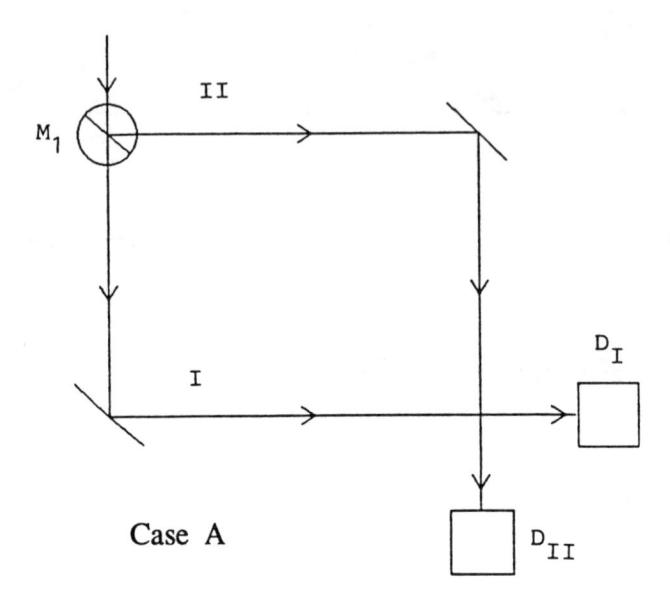

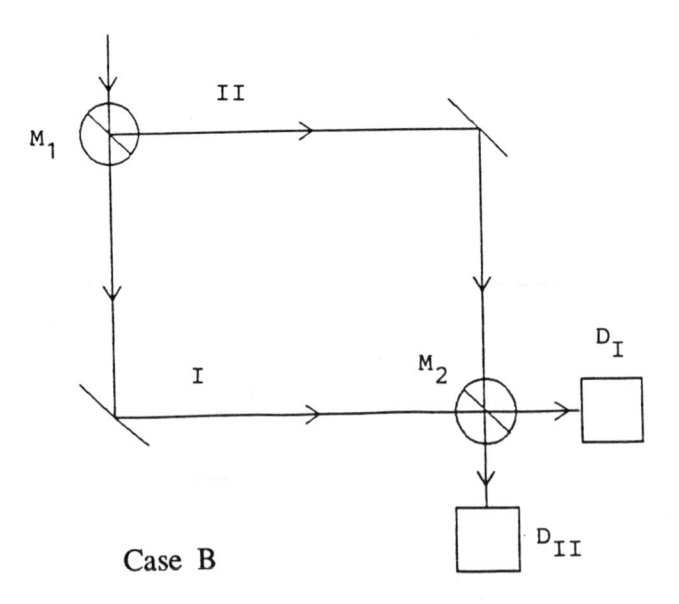

Case B

Fig. 2   Delayed choice experiment

Humberto R. Maturana

The Biological Foundations of Self Consciousness and the Physical Domain of Existence

1. Purpose
2. The problem
3. Nature of the answer
4. The scientific domain
    4.1 Scientific explanations
    4.2 Science
5. Objectivity in Parentheses
    5.1 An invitation
    5.2 Objectivity in parentheses
    5.3 The universum versus the multiversa
6. Basic notions
    6.1 Simple and composite unities
    6.2 Organization and structure
    6.3 Structure-determined systems
    6.4 Existence
    6.5 Structural coupling or adaptation
    6.6 Domain of existence
    6.7 Determinism
    6.8 Space
    6.9 Interactions
    6.10 Phenomenal domains
    6.11 Medium, niche, and environment
7. Basis for the answer: the living system
    7.1 Science deals only with structure-determined systems
    7.2 Regulation and control
    7.3 Living systems are structure-determined systems
    7.4 Determinism and prediction
    7.5 Ontogenic structural drift
    7.6 Structural intersection
    7.7 The living system
    7.8 Phylogenic structural drift
    7.9 Ontogenic possibilities
    7.10 Selection
8. The answer
    8.1 Cognition
    8.2 Language
9. Consequences
    9.1 Existence entails cognition
    9.2 There are as many cognitive domains as there are domains of existence
    9.3 Language is the human cognitive domain
    9.4 Objectivity
    9.5 Languaging: operation in a domain of structural coupling
    9.6 Language is a domain of descriptions
    9.7 Self-consciousness arises with language
    9.8 History
    9.9 The nervous system expands the domain of states of the living system
    9.10 Observing takes place in languaging
10. The domain of physical existence
11. Reality
12. Self-consciousness and reality

1. Purpose

My purpose in this essay is to explain cognition as a biological phenomenon, and to show, in the process, how self consciousness originates in language, revealing the ontological foundations of the physical domain of existence as a limiting cognitive domain. In order to do this, I shall start from two necessary experiential conditions that are at the same time my problem and my explanatory instruments, namely: a) that cognition, as is apparent from the fact that any alteration of the biology of our nervous system alters our cognitive capacities, is a biological phenomenon that must be explained as such; and b) that we, as this essay will demonstrate, exist as human beings in language, using language for our explanations. These two experiential conditions are my starting point because I must be in them in any explanatory attempt; they are my problem because I choose to explain them, and they are necessarily my instruments because I must use cognition and language in order to explain cognition and language.

I propose *not to take* cognition and language as given unexplainable properties, but to take them as phenomena of our human domain of experience that arise in the praxis of our living, and as such deserve explanation as biological phenomena. It is also my purpose to use our condition of existing in language to show how the physical domain of existence arises in language as a cognitive domain. I intend to show that the observer and observing, as biological phenomena, are ontologically primary with respect to the object and the physical domain of existence.

2. The problem

I shall take cognition as the fundamental problem, and I shall explain language in the process of explaining cognition. We human beings assess cognition in any domain by specifying the domain with a question and demanding adequate behavior or adequate action in that domain. If what we observe as an answer satisfies us as adequate behavior or as adequate action in the domain specified by the question, then we accept it as an expression of cognition in that domain, and claim that the person who answers our query knows. Thus, if someone claims to know algebra, that is, to be an algebrist, we demand of him or her to perform in the domain of what we consider algebra to be, and if according to us, she or he performs adequately in that domain, then we accept the claim. If the question asked is not answered with what we consider to be adequate behavior or adequate action in the domain that it specifies, the person being asked disintegrates or disappears, loses his or her class identity as an entity existing in the operational domain specified by the question, and the questioner proceeds henceforth according to his or her non-existence. In these circumstances, since adequate behavior (or adequate action) is the only criterion that we possess to assess cognition, I shall take adequate behavior or adequate action in any domain as this is specified by a question, as the phenomenon to be explained when explaining cognition.

3. Nature of the answer

I am a biologist, and it is from my experience as a biologist that in this essay I am treating the phenomenon of cognition as a biological phenomenon. Furthermore, since as a biologist I am a scientist, it is as a scientist that I shall provide a biological explanation of the phenomenon of cognition. To do this I shall make explicit what I consider to be adequate as a scientific explanation (*section 4*), so that all the implications of my explanation may be apparent to the reader, and she or he may know when an adequate scientific explanation is arrived at. I shall make explicit my epistemological standing with respect to the notion of objectivity (*section 5*), so that the ontological status of my explanation may be apparent. I shall also render explicit the notions that I use in my explanation by showing how they belong to our daily life (*section 6*), so as to show how we are involved as human beings in explanation. I shall specify the nature of the biological phenomena involved in my explanation (*section 7*), so that our involvement, as living systems in the explanation as well as in the phenomenon of cognition itself, may be apparent. Finally, in the process of explaining the phenomenon of cognition as a biological phenomenon, I shall show how it is that scientific theories arise as free creations of the human mind, how it is that they explain human experience rather than an independent objective world, and how the physical domain of existence arises in the explanation of the praxis of living of the observer, as a feature of the ontology of observing (*sections 8 to 11*).

4. The scientific domain

We find ourselves as human beings here and now in the praxis of living, in the happening of being human, in language languaging, in an *a priori* experiential situation in which everything that is, everything that occurs, is and occurs in us as part of our praxis of living. In these circumstances, whatever we say about how anything happens takes place in the praxis of our living as a comment, as a reflection, as a reformulation, in short, as an explanation of the praxis of our living, and as such it does not replace or constitute the praxis of living that it purports to explain. Thus, to say that we are made of matter, or to say that we are ideas in the mind of god, are both explanations of that which we live as our experience of being, yet neither matter nor ideas in the mind of god constitute the experience of being that they are supposed to explain. Explanations take place operationally in a meta-domain with respect to that which they explain.

Furthermore, in daily life, in the actual dynamics of human interactions, an explanation is always an answer to a question about the origin of a given phenomenon, and is accepted or rejected by a listener who accepts or rejects it according to whether it satisfies his or her particular implicit or explicit criterion of acceptability. For this reason, there are as many different kinds of explanations as there are criteria of acceptability for reformulations of the happening of living of the observers that the observers may specify. Accordingly, each domain of explanations, as it is defined by a particular criterion of acceptability, constitutes a closed cognitive domain as a domain of acceptable statements or actions for the observers who accept that particular criterion of acceptability. Science, modern science, as a cognitive domain is no exception to this. Indeed, modern science is that particular cognitive domain which takes what is called the scientific explanation as the criterion of validation (acceptability) of the statements that pertain to it. Let me make this explicit.

4.1 Scientific explanations

Scientists usually do not reflect upon the constitutive conditions of science. Yet it is possible to abstract, from what modern scientists do, an operational (and, hence, experiential) specification of what constitutes a scientific explanation as the criterion of validation of what they claim are their scientific statements. Furthermore, it is possible to describe this criterion of validation of scientific statements as a reformulation of what is usually called the scientific method.

Different domains of human activities entail different intentions. Thus, as the intention of art is to generate an aesthetic experience, and the intention of technology is to produce, the intention of science is to explain. It is, therefore, in the context of explaining that the criterion of validation of a scientific explanation is the conjoined satisfaction in the praxis of living of an observer of four operational conditions, one of which, the proposition of an *ad hoc* mechanism that generates the phenomenon explained as a phenomenon to be witnessed by the observer in his or her praxis of living, is the scientific explanation. And it is in the context of explaining that it must be understood that the scientific explanation is the criterion of validation of scientific statements. Finally, it is also in the context of explaining that it must be recognized that a modern scientific community is a community of observers (henceforth called standard observers) who use the scientific explanation as the criterion of validation of their statements. There are no such things as scientific observations, scientific hypotheses or scientific predictions: there are only scientific explanations and scientific statements. It also follows that the standard observer can make scientific statements in any domain of his or her praxis of living in which he or she can make scientific explanations.

As stated, a scientific statement is valid as a scientific statement only within the community of standard observers, who are defined as such because they can realize and accept the scientific explanation as the criterion of validation of their statements. This makes scientific statements consensual statements, and the community of standard observers a scientific community. That in principle any human being can belong to the scientific community is due to two facts of experience: one, it is as a living human being that an observer can realize and accept the scientific explanation as the criterion of validation of his or her statements and become a standard observer; the other, the criterion of validation of scientific statements is the operational criterion of validation of actions and statements in daily life, even if it is not used with greater precision in order to avoid confusion of phenomenal domains. Indeed, these two experiential facts constitute the basis for the claim of universality that scientists make for their statements, but what is peculiar in scientists is that they are careful to avoid confusion of phenomenal domains when applying the criterion of validation of scientific statements in the praxis of living.

Scientists and philosophers of science usually believe that the operational effectiveness of science and technology reveals an objective independent reality, and that scientific statements reveal the features of an independent universe, of an objective world. Many scientists and philosophers of science believe that without the independent existence of an objective reality science could not take place. Yet, if one makes a constitutive, an ontological analysis of the criterion of validation of scientific statements as I have done above, one can see that scientific explanations do not require the assumption of objectivity because scientific explanations do not explain an independent objective reality. Scientific explanations explain the praxis of living of the observer, and they do so with the operational coherences brought forth by the observer in his or her praxis of living. It is this fact which gives science its biological foundations and makes science a cognitive domain bound to the biology of the observer with characteristics that are determined by the ontology of observing.

4.2 Science

In conclusion, the operational description of what constitutes a scientific explanation as the criterion of validation of scientific statements reveals the following characteristics of scientific statements in general, and of science as a domain of scientific statements in particular. Scientific statements are consensual statements valid only within the community of standard observers who generate them, and science as the domain of scientific statements does not need an objective independent reality nor does it reveal one. Therefore, the operational effectiveness of science as a cognitive domain rests only on the operational coherence that exists in the praxis of living of the standard observers who generate it as a particular domain of consensual coordinations of actions in the praxis of their living together as a scientific community. Science is not a manner of revealing an independent reality, it is a manner of bringing forth a particular reality bound to the conditions that constitute the observer as a human being.

Since the members of a community of standard observers can generate scientific statements in any phenomenal domain of the praxis of living in which they can apply the criterion of validation of scientific statements, the universality of a particular body of scientific statements within the human domain will depend on the universality in the human domain of the standard observers who can generate such a body of scientific statements. Finally, scientific statements are valid only as long as the scientific explanations that support them are valid, and these are valid only as long as the four operational conditions that must be conjointly satisfied in their constitution are satisfied with respect to all the phenomena deduced in the praxis of living of the standard observers, within the domain of operational coherences specified by the proposed generative mechanism.

It is frequently said that scientific explanations are reductionist propositions, educing that they consist of expressing the phenomena to be explained in more basic terms. This view is inadequate. Scientific explanations are constitutively non-reductionist explanations because they consist in generative propositions and not in expressing the phenomena of one domain in phenomena of another. This is so because in a scientific explanation the phenomenon explained must arise as a result of the operation of the generative mechanism, and cannot be part of it. In fact, if the latter were the case, the explanatory proposition would be constitutively inadequate and would have to be rejected. The phenomenon explained and the phenomena proper to the generative mechanism constitutively pertain to non-intersecting phenomenal domains.

The generative mechanism in a scientific explanation is brought forth by a standard observer from his or her domain of experiences in his or her praxis of living as an *ad hoc* proposition which, in principle, requires no justification. Therefore, the components of the generative mechanism, as well as the phenomena proper to their operation, have a foundational character with respect to the phenomenon to be explained, and as such, their validity is in principle accepted *a priori*. Accordingly, every scientific domain as a domain of scientific statements is founded on basic experiential premises not justified in it, and constitutes, in the praxis of living of the standard observer, a domain of operational coherences brought forth in the operational coherences entailed in the generative mechanisms of the scientific explanations that validate it.

5. *Objectivity in Parentheses*

If one looks at the two shadows of an object which simultaneously partially intercepts the path of two different lights, one white and one red, and if one has trichromatic vision, then one sees that while the area of the shadow cast by the white light which is bathed in red light looks red, the area of shadow cast by the red light which receives white light looks blue-green. This experience is compelling and unavoidable, even if one knows that the area of shadow cast by the red light should look white or grey because it receives only white light. If one asks how it is that one sees blue-green where there is white light only, one is told by a reliable authority that the experience of the blue-green shadow is a chromatic illusion because there is no blue-green shadow to justify it as a perception. We live numerous experiences in our daily life that we class like this, as illusions or hallucinations rather than perceptions, claiming that they do not constitute the capture of an independent reality because we can disqualify them by resorting to the opinion of a friend whose authority we accept, or by relying upon a different sensory experience that we consider as a more acceptable perceptual criterion. In the experience itself, however, we cannot distinguish between an illusion, an hallucination or a perception: illusion, hallucination and perception are experientially indistinguishable. It is only through the use of a different experience as a meta-experiential authoritative criterion of distinction, either of the same observer or of somebody else subject to similar restrictions, that such a distinction is socially made. Our incapacity to distinguish experientially between what we commonly call illusion, hallucination or perception, is constitutive in us as living systems, and not a limitation of our present state of knowledge. The recognition of this should lead us to put a question mark on any perceptual certainty.

5.1 An invitation

The word perception comes from the Latin expression *per capire* which means by capturing, and carries the implicit understanding that to perceive is to capture the features of a world independent of the observer. This view assumes objectivity, and, hence, the possibility of knowing a world independent of the observer, as the ontological condition on which the distinction between illusion, hallucination and perception that it entails is based. Therefore, to question the operational validity in the biological domain of the distinction between illusion, hallucination and perception, is to question the ontological validity of the notion of objectivity in the explanation of the phenomenon of cognition. But how to proceed? Any reflexion or comment about how the praxis of living comes about is an explanation, a reformulation of what takes place. If this reformulation does not question the properties of the observer, if it takes for granted cognition and language, then it must assume the independent existence of what is known. If, on the other hand, this reformulation questions the properties of the observer, if it asks about how cognition and language arise, then it must accept the experiential indistinguishability between illusion, hallucination and perception, and take as constitutive that existence is dependent on the biology of the observer. Most philosophical traditions pertain to the first statement, assuming the independent existence of something, such as matter, energy, ideas, god, mind, spirit ... or reality. I invite the reader to adopt the second, and to take seriously the constitutive condition of the observer's biological condition with all the consequences that this constitutive condition entails.

5.2 Objectivity in parentheses

The assumption of objectivity is not needed for the generation of a scientific explanation. Therefore, in the process of being a scientist explaining cognition as a biological phenomenon, I shall proceed without using the notion of objectivity to validate what I say, that is, *I shall put objectivity in parentheses.* In other words, I shall go on using an object language because this is the only language that we have (and can have), and I shall use the experience of being in language as my starting point while I use language to explain cognition and language. *I shall not claim* that what I say is valid because there is an independent objective reality that validates it. I shall speak as a biologist, and as such, I shall use the criterion of validation of scientific statements to validate what I say, accepting that everything that takes place is brought forth by the observer in his or her praxis of living as a primary experiential condition, and that any explanation is secondary.

5.3 The universum versus the multiversa

The assumption of objectivity, objectivity without parentheses, entails the assumption that existence is independent of the observer, that there is an independent domain of existence, the *universum*, which is the ultimate reference for the validation of any explanation. With objectivity without parentheses things - entities - exist independent of the observer who distinguishes them, and it is this independent existence of things (entities, ideas) which specifies truth. Objectivity without parentheses entails unity and, in the long run, reductionism, because it entails reality as a single ultimate domain defined by independent existence. He or she who has access to reality is necessarily right in any dispute, and those who do not have such access are necessarily wrong. In the universum co-existence demands obedience to knowledge.

Contrary to all this, objectivity in parentheses entails accepting that existence is brought forth by the distinctions of the observer, that there are as many domains of existence as kinds of distinctions the observer performs: objectivity in parentheses entails the *multiversa*, entails the notion that existence is constitutively dependent on the observer, and that there are as many domains of truths as domains of existence she or he brings forth in her or his distinctions.

6. Basic notions

6.1 Simple and composite unities

The basic operation that an observer performs in the praxis of living is the operation of distinction. In this operation an observer brings forth a unity (an entity, a whole) as well as the medium in which it is distinguished, including in this latter aspect all the operational coherences which make the distinction of the unity possible in his or her praxis of living.

An observer may distinguish in the praxis of living two kinds of unities, simple and composite unities. A simple unity is one brought forth in an operation of distinction that constitutes it as a whole by specifying its properties as a collection of dimensions of interactions in the medium in which it is distinguished. A simple unity arises, defined and characterized by a collection of properties, as a matter of distinction in the praxis of living of the observer.

A composite unity is a unity distinguished as a simple unity which, through further operations of distinction, is broken down by the observer into components which, through their composition, would constitute the original simple unity in the domain in which it is distinguished. A composite unity, therefore, is operationally distinguished as a simple unity in a meta-domain with respect to the domain in which its components are distinguished because it results from an operation of composition. As a result, the components of a composite unity and its correlated simple unity are in a constitutive relation of mutual specification. Thus, the properties of a composite unity distinguished as a simple one entail the properties of the components that constitute it as such, and conversely, the properties of the components of a composite unity and their manner of composition determine the properties that characterize it as a simple unity when distinguished as such. Accordingly, there is no such thing as the distinction of a component independent of the unity that it integrates, nor can a simple unity distinguished as a composite one be broken down into an arbitrary set of components disposed in an arbitrary composition. Indeed, there is no such thing as a free component floating around independently of the composite unity that it integrates. Therefore, whenever we say that we treat a simple unity as a composite one, and we claim that we do so by distinguishing in it elements that when put together, do not regenerate the original unity, we are not, in fact, breaking down the unity that we believe we are breaking down, but another one, and the elements that we distinguish are not components of the composite unity which we say they are.

6.2 Organization and structure

A particular composite unity is characterized by the components and relations between components that constitute it as a composite unity, which can be distinguished in a meta-domain with respect to its components, as a particular simple unity of a certain kind. As such, a particular composite unity has both organization and structure. These can be characterized as follows:

a) The relations between components in a composite unity that make it a composite unity of a particular kind, specifying its class identity as a simple unity in a meta-domain with respect to its components, constitutes its organization. In other words: the organization of a composite unity is the configuration of static or dynamic relations between its components that specify its class identity as a composite unity which can be distinguished as a simple unity of a particular kind. Therefore, if the organization of a composite unity changes, the composite unity loses its class identity, i.e., it disintegrates. The organization of a composite unity is necessarily an invariant while it conserves its class identity, and *vice versa*.

b) In a composite unity, be it static or dynamic, the actual components plus the actual relations that take place between them while realizing it as a particular composite unity characterized by a particular organization, constitute its structure. In other words, the structure of a particular composite unity is the manner by which it is actually constituted through actual static or dynamic components and relations in a particular space, and a particular composite unity conserves its class identity only as long as its structure realizes in it the organization that defines its class identity. Therefore, in any particular composite unity, the configuration of relations between components which constitutes its organization must be realized in its structure as a subset of all the actual relations that hold between its components as actual entities interacting in the composition.

It follows from all this, that the characterization of the organization of a composite unity as a configuration of relations between components says nothing about the characteristics or properties of these, other than that they must satisfy the relations of the organization of the composite unity through their interactions in its composition. It also follows that the structure of a composite unity can change without it losing its class identity if the configuration of relations which constitutes its organization is conserved through such structural changes. At the same time, it also follows that if the organization of a composite unity is not conserved through its structural changes, the composite unity loses its class identity: it disintegrates, and something else appears in its stead. Therefore, a dynamic composite unity is a composite unity in continuous structural change with conservation of organization.

6.3 Structure-determined systems

Since the structure of a composite unity consists in its components and their relations, any change in a composite unity consists in a structural change, and arises in it at every instant necessarily determined by its structure at that instant through the operation of the properties of its components. Furthermore, the structural changes that a composite unity undergoes as a result of an interaction are also determined by the structure of the composite unity. This is so because such structural changes take place in the interplay of the properties of the components of the composite unity as they are involved in its composition. Therefore, an external agent which interacts with a composite unity only triggers, rather than determining in it a structural change. Since this is a constitutive condition for composite unities, nothing external to them can specify what happens in them: there are no instructive interactions for composite unities. Finally, and as a result of this latter condition, the structure of a composite unity also determines with which structural configurations of the medium it may interact. In general, then, everything which happens in a composite unity is a structural change, and every structural change occurs in a composite unity determined at every instant by its structure at that instant. This is so both for static and for dynamic composite unities, and the only difference between these is that dynamic composite unities are in a continuous structural change generated as part of their structural constitution in the context of their interactions, while static ones are not. It follows from all this that composite unities are structure-determined systems in the sense that everything that happens in them is determined by their structure. This can be systematically expressed by saying that the structure of composite unity determines it at every instant:

a) the domain of all the structural changes that it may undergo with conservation of organization (class identity) and adaptation at that instant; I call this domain the instantaneous domain of the possible changes of state of the composite unity.

b) the domain of all the structural changes that it may undergo with loss of organization and adaptation at that instant; I call this domain the instantaneous domain of the possible disintegrations of the composite unity.

c) the domain of all the different structural configurations of the medium that it admits at that instant in interactions that trigger in it changes of state; I call this domain the instantaneous domain of the possible perturbations of the composite unity.

d) the domain of all the different structural configurations of the medium that it admits at that instant in interactions that trigger in it its disintegration; I call this domain the instantaneous domain of the possible destructive interactions of the composite unity.

These four domains of structural determinism which characterize every structure-determined system at every instant are obviously not fixed, and they change as the structure of the structure-determined system changes in the flow of its own internal structural dynamics or as a result of its interactions. These general characteristics of structure-determined systems have several additional consequences of which I shall mention six. The first is that during the ontogeny of a structure-determined system, its four domains of structural determinism change, following a course contingent to its interactions and its own internal structural dynamics. The second is that some structure-determined systems have recurrent domains of structural determinism because they have recurrent structural configurations, while others do not because their structure changes in a nonrecurrent manner. The third is that, although the structure of a structure-determined system determines the structural configurations of the medium with which it may interact, all its interactions arise as coincidences with independent systems that cannot be predicted from it. The fourth is that a composite unity exists only while it moves through the medium in interactions which are perturbations, and that it disintegrates at the first destructive interaction. The fifth is that, since the medium cannot specify what happens in a structure-determined system because it only triggers the structural changes that occur in this as a result of its interactions, all that can happen to a composite unity, in relation to its interactions in the medium, is that the course followed by its structural changes is contingent to the sequence of these interactions. The sixth is that, since mechanistic systems are structure-determined systems, and since scientific explanations entail the proposition of mechanistic systems as the systems that generate the phenomena to be explained in scientific explanations, we deal only with structure-determined systems.

6.4 Existence

By putting objectivity in parentheses we accept that constitutively we cannot claim the independent existence of things (entities, unities, ideas, etc.), and we recognize that a unity exists only in its distinction in the praxis of living of the observer that brings it forth. But we also recognize that the distinction takes place in the praxis of living of the observer in an operation that specifies simultaneously the class identity of the unity distinguished, either as a simple unity or as a composite one, and its domain of existence as the domain of the operational coherences in which its distinction makes sense also as a feature of his or her praxis of living. Since the class identity of a composite unity is defined by its organization, and since this can be realized in a composite unity only while this interacts in a domain of perturbations, existence in a composite unity entails the conservation of its organization as well as the conservation of its operational structural correspondence in the domain of operational coherences in which it is distinguished. Similarly, since the class identity of a simple unity is defined by its properties, and since these are defined in relation to the operational domain in which it is distinguished, existence in a simple unity entails the conservation of the properties that define it and the operational structural correspondence in which these properties are realized.

6.5 Structural coupling or adaptation

I call structural coupling or adaptation the relation of dynamic structural correspondence with the medium in which a unity conserves its class identity (organization in the case of a composite unity, and operation of its properties in the case of a simple one), and which is entailed in its distinction as it is brought forth by the observer in his or her praxis of living. Therefore, conservation of class identity and conservation of adaptation are constitutive conditions of existence for any unity (entity, system, whole, etc.) in the domain of existence in which it is brought forth by the observer in his or her praxis of living. As constitutive conditions of existence for any unity, conservation of class identity and conservation of adaptation are paired conditions of existence that entail each other so that if one is lost the other is lost, and the unity exists no more. When this happens, a composite unity disintegrates and a simple unity disappears.

6.6 Domain of existence

The operation of distinction that brings forth and specifies a unity, also brings forth and specifies its domain of existence as the domain of the operational coherences entailed by the operation of the properties through which the unity is characterized in its distinction. In other words, the domain of existence of a simple unity is the domain of operational validity of the properties that define it as such, and the domain of existence of a composite unity is the domain of operational validity of the properties of the components that constitute it. Furthermore, the constitutive operational coherence of a domain of existence as the domain of operational validity of the properties of the entities that define it, entails all that such validity requires. Accordingly, a simple unity exists in a single domain of existence specified by its properties, and a composite unity exists in two, in the domain of existence specified by its properties as it is distinguished as a simple unity, and in the domain of existence specified by the properties of its components as it is distinguished as a composite one. The entailment in the distinction of a unity, of its domain of existence as the domain of all the operational coherences - in the praxis of living of the observer - in which it conserves class identity and adaptation, is a constitutive condition of existence of every unity. A unity cannot exist outside its domain of existence, and if we imagine a unity outside its domain of existence, the one we imagine exists in a different domain from the unity that we claim we imagine.

6.7 Determinism

To say that a system is deterministic is to say that it operates according to the operational coherences of its domain of existence. And this is so because, due to our constitutive inability to experientially distinguish between what we commonly call perception and illusion, we cannot make any claim about an objective reality. This we acknowledge by putting objectivity in parentheses. In other words, to say that a system is deterministic is to say that all its changes are structural changes arising in it through the operation of the properties of its components in their interactions, and not through instructive processes in which an external agent specifies what happens in it. Accordingly, an operation of distinction that brings forth a simple unity brings forth its domain of existence as the domain of operational applicability of its properties, and constitutes the simple unity and its domain of existence as a deterministic system. At the same time, the operation of distinction that brings forth a composite unity brings forth its domain of existence as a domain of determinism in terms of the operational applicability of the properties that characterize its components, in the praxis of living of the observer. Accordingly, the operation of distinction that brings forth a composite unity brings forth both the composite unity and its domain of existence together, as deterministic systems in the corresponding domains of operational coherences of the praxis of living of the observer.

6.8 Space

The distinction of a unity brings forth its domain of existence as a space of distinctions whose dimensions are specified by the properties of the unities whose distinction entail it as a domain of operational coherences in the praxis of living of the observer. Thus, a simple unity exists and operates in a space specified by its properties, and a composite unity exists and operates in a space specified by its properties as a simple unity if distinguished as such, and in a space specified by the properties of its components if distinguished as a composite one. Accordingly, as a simple unity exists and operates in a single space, a composite unity exists and operates in two. Finally, it follows that without the distinction of a unity there is no space, and that the notion of a unity out of space, as well as the notion of an empty space, are non-sensical. A space is a domain of distinctions.

6.9 Interactions

Two simple unities interact when, as a result of the interplay of their properties, and in a manner determined by such interplay, they change their relative position in a common space or domain of distinctions. A composite unity interacts when some of its components, as a result of their interactions as simple unities with other simple unities that are not its components, change their manner of composing it, and it undergoes a structural change. It follows that a simple unity interacts in a single space - in the space that its properties define - and that a composite unity interacts in two, in the space defined by its properties as a simple unity, and in the space that its components define through their properties, also as simple unities, as they constitute its structure.

6.10 Phenomenal domains

A space is constituted in the praxis of living of the observer when he or she performs a distinction. The constitution of a space brings forth a phenomenal domain as the domain of distinctions of the relations and interactions of the unities that the observer distinguishes as populating that space. A simple unity operates in a single phenomenal domain, the phenomenal domain constituted through the operation of its properties as a simple unity. A composite unity operates in two phenomenal domains, the phenomenal domain constituted through the operation of its properties as a simple unity, and the phenomenal domain constituted through the operation of the properties of its components, which is where its composition takes place. Furthermore, the two phenomenal domains in which a composite unity operates do not intersect and cannot be reduced, one to the other, because there is a generative relation between them. The phenomenal domain, in which a composite unity operates as a simple unity, is secondary to the composition of the composite unity and constitutes a metaphenomenal domain with respect to the phenomenal domain in which the composition takes place. Due to this, a composite unity cannot participate as a simple unity in its own composition.

6.11 Medium, niche, and environment

I call the *medium* of a unity the containing background of distinctions, including all that is not involved in the unity's structure if it is a composite one, with respect to which an observer distinguishes it in his or her praxis of living, and in which it realizes its domain of existence. The medium includes both, that part of the background distinguished by the observer as surrounding the unity, and that part of the background the observer conceives as interacting with it, and which it obscures in its operation in structural coupling (in its domain of existence). I call this latter part of the medium, operationally defined moment by moment in its encounter with the medium in structural coupling, the *niche* of the unity. Accordingly, a unity continuously realizes and specifies its niche by actually operating in its domain of perturbations while conserving adaptation in the medium. As a consequence, the niche of a unity is not a fixed part of the medium in which a unity is distinguished, nor does it exist independent of the unity that specifies it; it changes as the domain of interactions of the unity changes (if it is a composite one) in its dynamics of structural change. In these circumstances, an observer can distinguish the niche of a unity, regardless of whether this is simple or composite, only by the use of the unity as its indicator. Finally, I call the *environment* of a unity all that an observer distinguishes as surrounding it. In other words, while the niche is that part of the medium that a unity encounters (interacts with) in its operation in structural coupling and obscures with its presence from the view of the observer, the environment is that part of the medium that an observer sees around a unity. Thus, a dynamic composite unity (like a living system), as it is distinguished in the praxis of living of the observer, is seen by this in an environment as an entity with a changing niche that it specifies, while it slides through the medium in continuous structural change with conservation of class identity and adaptation. A composite unity in its medium is like a tightrope walker, who moves on a rope in a gravitational field, and conserves his or her balance (adaptation) while her or his shape (structure) changes in a manner congruent with the visual and gravitational interactions he or she undergoes while walking (realizing its niche), and falls when this is no longer the case.

7. Basis for the answer: the living system

The answer to the question of cognition requires that we now reflect upon the constitution and operation of living systems, and that we take into account some additional epistemological and ontological considerations about the conditions that our understanding of the systems must satisfy.

7.1 Science deals only with structure-determined systems

To the extent that a scientific explanation entails the proposition of a structure-determined system as the mechanism that generates the phenomenon to be explained, we as scientists can deal only with structure-determined systems, and we cannot handle systems that change in a manner specified by the external agents that impinge upon them. Accordingly, whatever I say about living systems will be said on the understanding, that all the phenomena to which they give rise, arise through their operation as structure-determined systems in a domain of existence brought forth by the observer in her or his distinction also as a structure-determined system.

7.2 Regulation and control

As I have indicated in section 6.10, the distinction of a composite unity entails the distinction in the praxis of living of the observer of two phenomenal domains, that do not intersect because the operation of a composite unity as a simple one is secondary to its composition. As a result, the whole cannot operate as its own component, and a component cannot operate in lieu of the whole that it integrates. In these circumstances, notions of control or regulation do not denote actual operations in the composition of a composite unity, because this takes place only through the realization, in the presence of the properties of its components in their actual interactions. Notions of regulation and control only denote relations taking place in a descriptive domain as the observer relates mappings in language of his or her distinctions of a whole and its components in his or her praxis of living.

7.3 Living systems are structure-determined systems

In order to explain the phenomenon of cognition as a biological phenomenon, I must treat living systems as structure-determined systems. I consider that to do so is legitimate for at least three reasons. The first is an operational one: we know as a feature of our praxis of living, that any structural change in a living system results in a change in its characteristics and properties, and that similar structural changes in different members of the same species, result in similar changes in their characteristics and properties. The second is an epistemological one: if we do not treat living systems as structure-determined systems, we cannot provide scientific explanations for the phenomena proper to them. The third is an ontological one: the only systems that we can explain scientifically are structure-determined systems, therefore, if I provide a scientific explanation of the phenomenon of cognition in living systems, I provide a proof that living systems are structure-determined systems in our praxis of living as standard observers, which is where we distinguish them.

7.4 Determinism and prediction

The fact that a structure-determined system is deterministic does not mean that an observer should be able to predict the course of its structural changes. Determinism and predictability pertain to different operational domains in the praxis of living of the observer. Determinism is a feature that characterizes a system in terms of the operational coherences that constitute it, and in terms of its domain of existence, as it is brought forth in the operations of distinction of the observer. Accordingly, there are as many different domains of determinism as domains of different operational coherences the observer brings forth in her or his domain of experiences. A prediction, however, is a computation that an observer makes of the structural changes of a structure-determined system, as she or he follows the consequences of the operation of the properties of the components of the system in the realization of the domain of determinism that these properties constitute. As such, a prediction can only take place after the observer has completely described the system as a structure that is determined in terms of the operational coherences that constitute it in his or her domain of experiences. Therefore, the success or failure of a prediction only reflects the ability or inability of an observer to confuse or not to confuse phenomenal domains in his or her praxis of living, and indeed, to make the computation that constitutes the prediction in the phenomenal domain where he or she claims to make it.

In these circumstances, there are two occasions when an observer, dealing with a structure-determined system that does not confuse phenomenal domains, will not be able to predict its structural changes. One occasion is when an observer knows that she or he is dealing with a structure determined by experience in the praxis of living with its components, but cannot encompass it in his or her descriptions, and, thus, cannot effectively treat it as such in its domain of existence, nor compute its changes of state. The other occasion is when an observer in his or her praxis of living aims at characterizing the present unknown state of a system, assumed to be structure-determined, by interacting with some of its components. By doing this, the observer triggers in the system an unpredictable change of state which he or she then uses to characterize its initial state and to predict in it a later one within the domain of determinism specified by the properties of its components.

Therefore, since the domain of determinism of a structure-determined system, as the domain of operational coherences of its components, is brought forth in its distinction in the praxis of living of the observer, and since, in order to compute a change of state in a system, the observer must determine its present state through an interaction with its components, any attempt to compute a change of state in a structure-determined system entails a necessary uncertainty due to the manner of determination of its initial state within the constraints of the operational coherences of its domain of existence. This predictive uncertainty may vary in magnitude in different domains of distinctions, but it is always present because it is constitutive of the phenomenon of cognition as a feature of the ontology of observing, and not of an objective independent reality. With this I am also saying, that the uncertainty principle of physics pertains to the ontology of observing, and that it does not characterize an independent universe because, as I shall show further on, the physical domain of existence is a cognitive domain brought forth in the praxis of living of the observer, by the observer as an explanation of his or her praxis of living.

7.5 Ontogenic structural drift

It is said that a boat is drifting when it is floating on the sea without rudder or oars, following a course generated moment after moment in its encounter with the waves and wind that impinge upon it, and which lasts as long as the boat continues to float (conserves adaptation) and keeps the shape of a boat (conserves organization). As such a drifting boat follows a course, without alternatives, which is deterministically generated moment after moment in its encounters with the waves and the wind. As a consequence of this, a drifting boat is also always, and at any moment, in the only place where it can be, in a present that is continuously emerging from the sequence of its interactions in the drift. The deterministic process, which generates the course followed by a drifting boat, takes place as a feature of the structural dynamics of the structure-determined system constituted by the boat, the wind, and the waves, as these are brought forth by the observer in his or her praxis of living. Therefore, if an observer cannot predict the course of a drifting boat, it is not because his or her distinction of the boat, the wind, and the waves, in his or her domain of experiences, does not entail a structure-determined system in which the course followed by the boat arises in a deterministic manner, but because he or she cannot encompass in his or her description of the interactions between the boat, the wind, and the waves, the whole structure of the structure-determined system in which the course followed by the boat is a feature of its changes of structure.

What happens with the generation of course followed by a drifting boat, is the general case for the generation of the course followed by the structural changes of the structure-determined system which the observer distinguishes in his or her praxis of living, as it interacts in the medium, as if with an independent entity with conservation of class identity (organization) and adaptation (structural coupling). Since living systems are dynamic structure-determined systems, this applies to them, and the ontogeny of a living system, as its history of structural changes with conservation of organization and adaptation, is its ontogenic structural drift. All that applies to the course followed by a drifting boat, applies to the course followed by the structural changes that take place in the ontogeny of a living system and to the course followed by the displacement of a living system in the medium during its ontogeny.

Let me make this clear. In general terms, a drift is the course followed by the structural changes of a structure-determined system, which arises moment after moment generated in the interactions of the system with another independent system, while its relation of correspondence (adaptation) with this other system (medium) and its organization (class identity) remain invariant. According to this, the individual life history of a living system, as a history of continuous structural changes triggered in it by its recurrent interactions with the medium as an independent entity, and which lasts as long as its organization and adaptation are conserved, takes place as a structural drift. Similarly, since the course of the displacement of a living system in the medium is generated moment after moment as a result of its interactions with the medium as an independent entity while its organization and adaptation are conserved, the displacement of a living system in the medium while it realizes its niche takes place as a drift. Living systems exist in continuous structural and positional drift (ontogenic drift), while they are alive as a matter of constitution.

As is the case with a drifting boat, at any given moment, a living system is where it is in the medium and has the structure that it has, as the present of its ontogenic drift in a deterministic manner, and could not be anywhere other than where it is, nor could it have a structure different from the one that it has. The many different paths that an observer may consider possible for a drifting boat to follow at any instant, or the many different ontogenic courses that an observer may consider for a living system at any moment, are possible only as imagined alternatives in the description of what would happen in each case, if the conditions were different, and are not actual alternatives in the course of the boat or in the ontogeny of the living system. A drift as a process of change, and as is the case with all processes of change in structure-determined systems, courses without alternatives in the domain of determinism in which it is brought forth by the distinctions of the observer. Indeed, such imagined alternatives are imaginable only from the perspective of the observer's inability to treat the boat, the wind and the waves, or the living system and the medium that he or she brings forth in his or her praxis of living, as structure-determined systems whose changes of structure he or she computes. If we are serious about our explanations as scientists, then we must accept as an ontological feature of our activity as observers, that every entity we bring forth in our distinctions, is where it is and has the structure that it has, in the only manner possible, given the domain of operational coherences (domain of determinism) that we also bring forth as its domain of existence in its distinction.

Finally, let me mention several implications of all this for the entities that we bring forth as living systems in our praxis of living:

a) Since, for a living system a history of interactions without disintegration can only be a history of perturbations, i.e., a history of interactions in the niche, a living system, while living, necessarily slides in ontogenic drift through the medium in the realization of its niche. This means that aim, goal, purpose or intention, do not enter into the realization of a living system as a structure-determined system.

b) Since the structure of a living system is continuously changing, both through its internal dynamics and through the structural changes triggered in it in its interactions with operationally independent entities, the niche of a living system (the feature of the medium that it actually encounters in its interactions) is necessarily continuously changing, congruent with the continuous structural drift of the living system while this remains alive. Furthermore, this is so, regardless of whether the observer considers that the environment of the living system changes or remains constant. This means that as an observer brings forth a living system in her or his praxis of living, this may appear to her or him as continuously changing in its use of a constant environment, or, conversely, as unchanging in a continuously changing environment, because the observer cannot see the encounter of a living system and its niche, which is where conservation of adaptation takes place.

c) Conservation of adaptation does not mean that the manner of living of a living system remains invariant. It means that a living system has an ontogeny only while it conserves its class identity and its dynamic structural correspondence with the medium as it undergoes its interactions, and that there is no constitutive restriction about the magnitude of its moment-by-moment structural changes other than that they should take place within the constraints of its structural determinism and its conservation of organization and adaptation. Indeed, I could speak of the laws of conservation of organization and adaptation as ontological conditions for the existence of any structure-determined system in the same manner as physicists speak of the laws of conservation in physics as ontological conditions for the occurence of physical phenomena.

Every living system, including us observers, is at any moment where it is, has the structure that it has, and does what it does at that moment, always in a structural and relational situation that is the present of an ontogenic drift which starts at its inception as such in a particular place with a particular structure, and follows the only course that it can follow. Different kinds of living systems differ in the spectrum of ontogenies, which an observer can consider possible for each of them in his or her discourse, as a result of their different initial structures and different starting places, but each ontogeny that takes place does so as a unique ontogenic drift in a process without alternatives.

7.6 Structural intersection

When an observer brings forth a composite unity in his or her praxis of living, he or she brings forth an entity in which the configuration of relations between components that constitute its organization, is a subset of all the actual relations that take place between its components, as these realize its structure and constitute it as a whole in the domain of existence in which they are brought forth (see section 6.2). As such, the organization of a composite unity does not exhaust the relations and interactions in which the components that realize it may participate in their domain of existence. The result of this is that in the structural realization of a composite unity, its components may participate, through properties other than those that involve them in the realization of its organization, in the realization of the organization of many other composite unities which intersect structurally with it. Furthermore, when the components of a composite unity are themselves composite unities, these may participate in structural intersections that take place through the components of its components. In any case, when an observer distinguishes two or more structurally intersecting systems, he or she distinguishes two or more different composite unities realized through the same body.

Structurally intersecting systems exist and operate as simple unities in different phenomenal domains specified by their different organizations. Yet, depending on how their structural intersection takes place, structurally intersecting composite unities may exist as such in the same or different domains of existence. Thus, when two composite unities structurally intersect through their components, they share components and have as composite unities the same domain of existence. But when two composite unities structurally intersect through the components of the components of one or both, they do not share components and as composite unities have different domains of existence. Nevertheless, since in a structural intersection there are components of components of components, simultaneously participating in the structure of several systems, structural changes that take place in one of several structurally intersecting systems as part of its ontogenic drift, may give rise to structural changes in the other intersecting systems, and thus participate in their otherwise independent ontogenic drifts. In other words, structurally intersecting systems are structurally interdependent because, either through the intersection of their domains of structural determinism, or through the intersection of the domains of structural determinism of their components, or through both, they affect each other's structures in the course of their independently generated structural changes, and although they may exist as composite unities in different domains, their ontogenic drifts intersect, forming a network of co-ontogenic drifts.

Thus, an observer may distinguish, in the structural realization of a human being as a living system, the simultaneous or successive intersection of a mammal, a person, a woman, a doctor, and a mother, all of which are different composite unities defined by different organizations which are simultaneously or successively conserved while they are realized in their different domains of existence, with particular characteristics resulting from the continuous braiding of their different ontogenic drifts through the continuous interplay of their structural changes.

Furthermore, these structural intersections result in dependent domains of disintegrations as well as dependent domains of conservations which need not be reciprocal, when the conservation of one class identity entails the conservation of structural features that are involved in the conservation of another. For example, in the structural intersection of a student and a human being in a living system, the conservation of the class identity *student* entails the conservation of the class identity *human being*, but not the reverse: the disintegration of the student does not entail the disintegration of the human being, but the disintegration of the human being carries with it the disintegration of the student. Also, a particular composite unity may disintegrate through different kinds of structural changes, like disintegrating as a student through failing an examination or through attaining the final degree, with different consequences in the network of structural intersections to which it belongs.

The structural intersection of systems does not mean that the same system is viewed in different ways from different perspectives, since, due to their different organizations, structural intersecting systems exist in different phenomenal domains and are realized through different structural dynamics. It only means that the elements which realize a particular composite unity as its components through some of their properties as simple unities, participate, through other of their properties as simple unities, as components of other unities that exist as legitimately different ones because they have different domains of disintegrations. The interactions and relations, in which the components of a system participate through dimensions other than those through which they constitute it, I call orthogonal interactions and relations, and it is through these that structurally intersecting systems may exist in non-intersecting phenomenal domains and yet have uni-directional or reciprocal relations of structural dependency. Finally, it is also through the orthogonal interactions of their components that structurally independent systems which exist in non-intersecting phenomenal domains may also have co-ontogenic drifts.

7.7 The living system

In 1970 I proposed that living systems were dynamic systems constituted as autonomous unities by being closed circular concatenations (closed networks) of molecular productions in which the different kinds of molecules that composed them participated in the production of each other, and in which everything could change in the manner in which they were realized, except for the closed circularity that constituted them as unities (see Maturana 1970, in

Maturana and Varela 1980). In 1973 Francisco Varela and I expanded this characterization of living systems: first, a composite unity whose organization can be described as a closed network of productions of components, which through their interactions constitute the network of productions that produce them and specify its extension by constituting its boundaries in their domain of existence, is an autopoietic system. Second, a living system is an autopoietic system whose components are molecules. We proposed that living systems are molecular autopoietic systems, and that as such they exist in the molecular space as closed networks of molecular productions that specify their own limits (see Maturana and Varela 1973, in Maturana and Varela 1980, and Maturana 1975). Nothing is said about thermodynamic constraints in this description of the molecular constitution of living systems as autopoietic systems. This is so because the realization of living systems as molecular systems entails the satisfaction of such constraints. In fact, the statement that a composite unity exists as such in the domain of existence of its components implies the satisfaction of the conditions of existence of these.

7.7.1 Implications

The recognition that living systems are molecular autopoietic systems carries with it several implications and consequences.

a) Living systems as autopoietic systems are structure-determined systems, and everything that applies to these applies to them. In particular, this means that everything that occurs in a living system takes place in it in the actual operation of the properties of its components through relations of neighbourhood (relations of contiguity) constituted in these very same operations. According to this, notions of regulation and control do not and cannot reflect actual operations in the structural realization of a living system because they do not denote actual relations of neighborhood in it. These notions only reveal relations that the observer establishes when he or she compares different moments in the course of transformations of the network of processes that take place in the structural realization of a particular living system. Therefore, the only peculiar thing about living systems as structure-determined systems is that they are molecular autopoietic systems.

b) Autopoiesis is a dynamic process that takes place in the ongoing flow of occurrence, and cannot be grasped in a static instantaneous view of distribution of components. For this reason, a living system exists only through the continuous structural transformation entailed in its autopoiesis, and only while this is conserved in the constitution of its ontogeny. This has two basic results: one is that living systems can be realized through many different changing dynamic structures, the other is that in the generation of lineages through reproduction, living systems are constitutively open to continuous phylogenic structural change.

c) A living system either exists as a dynamic structure-determined system in structural coupling in the medium in which it is brought forth by the observer, i.e., in a relation of conservation of adaptation through its continuous structural change in the realization of its niche, or it does not exist. A living system, while living, is necessarily in a dynamic relation of correspondence with the medium through its operation in its domain of existence, and to live is to glide through a domain of perturbations in an ontogenic drift that takes place through the realization of an ever-changing niche.

d) A living system as a structure-determined system operates only in the present of the structural realization of its autopoiesis in the molecular space, and as such it is necessarily open to the flow of molecules through it. At the same time, a living system as an autopoietic system operates only by generating states in autopoiesis, otherwise it disintegrates; due to this, living systems are closed systems with respect to the dynamics of their states.

7.7.2 Consequences

a) To the extent that a living system is a structure-determined system, and everything in it takes place through neighbourhood relations between its components in the present of the operation of their properties, notions of purpose and goal, which imply that at every instant a later state of a system as a whole operates as part of its structure in the present, do not apply to living systems and cannot be used to characterize their operation. A living system may appear to operate as a purposeful or goal-directed system only to an observer who, having seen the ontogeny of other living systems of the same kind in the same circumstances in his or her praxis of living, confuses phenomenal domains by putting the consequences of its operation as a whole among the processes that constitute it.

b) Because living systems are structure-determined systems, there is no inside or outside in their operation as autopoietic unities; they are in autopoiesis as closed wholes in their dynamics of states, or they disintegrate. Due to this, living systems do not use or misuse an environment in their operation as autopoietic unities, nor do they make mistakes in their ontogenic drifts. In fact, a living system in its operation in a medium with conservation of organization and adaptation as befit it as a structure-determined system, brings forth its ever changing niche as it realizes itself in its domain of existence as a background of operational coherences which it does not distinguish and with which it does not interact.

c) Living systems necessarily form, through their recurrent interactions with each other as well as with the non-biotic medium, co-ontogenic and co-phylogenic systems of braided structural drifts that last as long as they conserve their autopoiesis through the conservation of their reciprocal structural couplings. Such is biological evolution. As a result, every living system, including us human beings as observers, is always found in the spontaneous realization of its domain of existence in congruence with a biotic and a non-biotic medium. Every living system is, at every instant, as it is and where it is, a node of a network of co-ontogenic drifts, that necessarily involves all the entities with which it interacts in the domain in which it is brought forth by the observer in his or her praxis of living. As a consequence, an observer as a living system can only distinguish an entity as a node of the network of co-ontogenic drifts to which it belongs and where it exists in structural coupling.

d) The only thing peculiar to living systems is that they are autopoietic systems in the molecular space. In these circumstances, a given phenomenon is a biological phenomenon only to the extent that its realization entails the realization of the autopoiesis of at least one autopoietic system in the molecular space.

e) Modern procariotic and eucariotic cells are typical autopoietic systems in the molecular space, and because their autopoiesis is not the result of their being composed by more basic autopoietic subsystems, I call them first-order autopoietic systems. I call second-order autopoietic systems those whose autopoiesis is the result of their being composed of more basic autopoietic unities. Organisms such as multicellular systems are an example. Yet organisms may also "be," and I think that most of them actually are, first-order autopoietic systems as closed networks or molecular productions involving intercellular processes as much as intracellular ones. Accordingly, an organism would exist as such in the structural intersection of a first-order autopoietic system with a second-order one, both realized through the autopoiesis of the cells that compose the latter. The same happened originally with the eucariotic cell as this arose through the endosymbiosis of procariotic ones (Margoulis).

f) An organism such as a second-order autopoietic system, is an ectocellular symbiont composed of cells, usually of common origin but not always so, that constitute it through their co-ontogenic drift. An organism such as a first-order autopoietic system, however, is not composed of cells even though its realization depends upon the realization of the autopoiesis of the cells that intersect structurally with it as they constitute it in their co-ontogenic drift. The first- and second-order autopoietic systems which intersect structurally in the realization of an organism exist in different non-intersecting phenomenal domains.

7.8 Phylogenic structural drift

Reproduction is a process in which a system gives origin, through its fracture, to systems characterized by the same organization (class identity) that characterized the original one, but with structures that vary with respect to it (Maturana 1980). A reproductive phylogeny or lineage is a succession of systems generated through sequential reproductions that conserve a particular organization. Accordingly, each particular reproductive lineage or phylogeny is defined by the particular organization conserved through the sequential reproductions that constitute it. Therefore, a reproductive phylogeny or lineage lasts only as long as the organization which defines it is conserved, regardless of how much the structure that realizes this organization in each successive member of the lineage changes with each reproductive step (see Maturana 1980, and Maturana and Varela 1984).

It follows that a reproductive phylogeny or lineage as a succession of ontogenic drifts, constitutively occurs as a drift of the structures that realize the organization conserved along it. It also follows that each of the reproductive steps which constitute a reproductive phylogeny is the occasion that opens the possibility for a discrete, large or small, change in the course of its structural drift. As such, a reproductive phylogeny or lineage comes to an end through the structural changes of its members. And this occurs either because autopoiesis is lost after the last of them, or because through the conservation of autopoiesis in the offspring, a particular set of relations of the drifting structure begins to be conserved, through the following sequential reproductions, as the organization that defines and starts a new lineage. This has several general implications of which I shall mention only a few:

a) A member of a reproductive phylogeny either stays in structural coupling (conserves adaptation) in its domain of existence until its reproduction, and the phylogeny continues; or it disintegrates before then and the phylogeny continues; or it disintegrates before then and the phylogeny ends with it.

b) A living system is a member of the reproductive phylogeny in which it arises only if it conserves through its ontogeny the organization that defines the phylogeny, and continues the phylogeny only if such organization is conserved through its reproduction.

c) Many different reproductive phylogenies can be conserved operationally embedded in each other, forming a system of nested phylogenies, if there is an intersection of the structural realization of the different organizations that define them. When this happens there is always a fundamental reproductive phylogeny whose realization is necessary for the realization of all the others. This has occurred in the evolution of living systems in the form of the phylogenic drift of a system of branching nested reproductive phylogenies in which the fundamental reproductive phylogeny is that in which autopoiesis is conserved (see Maturana 1980, and Maturana and Varela 1984). Thus, the system of branching phylogenies defined by the conservation of autopoiesis through reproductive cells in eucariotic organisms, has carried, embedded in it through the structural intersection of their realizations, many staggered nested organizations that characterize the coincident lineages conserved through it. This we recognize in the many nested taxonomic categories that we distinguish in any organism when we classify it. For example, a human being is a vertebrate, a mammal, a primate, *Homo*, *Homo sapiens*, all of which are different categories corresponding to different systems of partially overlapping phylogenies conserved together through the conservation of its autopoiesis.

d) The ontogenic drifts of the members of a reproductive phylogeny take place in reciprocal structural coupling with many different and continuously changing living and non-living systems that form part of the medium in which they realize their niches. As a result, every individual ontogeny in living systems follows a course embedded in a system of co-ontogenies that constitutes a network of co-phylogenic structural drifts. This can be generalized by saying that evolution is constitutively a co-evolution, and that every living system is at any moment where it is and has the structure that it has, as an expression of the present of the domain of operational coherences constituted by the network of co-phylogenic structural drifts to which it belongs. As a result, the operational coherences of each living system, in its present, necessarily entails the operational coherences of the whole biosphere.

e) The observer as a living system is not an exception to all that has been said above. Due to this, an observer can only make distinctions that, as operations in his or her praxis of living, take place as operations in the present of the domain of operational coherences constituted by the network of co-ontogenic and co-phylogenic structural drifts to which he or she belongs.

7.9 Ontogenic possibilities

The ontogeny of every structure-determined system starts with an initial structure which is the structure that realizes the system in its inception. In living systems such initial structure is a cellular unity that may originate, either as a single cell or as a small multicellular entity through a reproductive fracture from a cellular maternal system whose organization it conserves, or as a single cell *de novo* from noncellular elements. In every living system its initial structure constitutes the structural starting point that specifies in it what an observer sees as the configuration of all the courses of ontogenic drifts that it may undergo under different circumstances of interactions in the medium. As a result, that which constitutes a lineage in living systems is the conservation through their reproduction of a particular initial structure that specifies a particular configuration of possible ontogenic drifts. What constitutes the organization conserved through reproduction that specifies the identity of the lineage, is that configuration. Accordingly, a lineage comes to an end when the configuration of possible ontogenic drifts that defines it stops being conserved.

I call the configuration of possible ontogenic drifts which specifies a lineage through its conservation, the ontogenic phenotype of the lineage. In each particular living system, however, only one of the ontogenic courses considered by the observer to be possible in the ontogenic phenotype is realized as a result of its internal dynamics under the contingencies of the particular perturbations that it undergoes in its domain of existence with conservation of organization and adaptation. Consequently, different composite unities may have different or similar ontogenic structural drifts under different or similar histories of perturbations in their domains of existence, only within the domain of possibilities set by their different or similar initial structures. Indeed, nothing can happen in the ontogeny of a living system as a composite unity that is not permitted in its initial structure. In other words and with the understanding that the initial structure of a living system is its genetic constitution, it is apparent that nothing can happen in the ontogenic structural drift of a living system that is not allowed in its genetic constitution as a feature of its possible ontogenies.

With this understanding, it is also apparent that nothing is determined in the initial structure or genetic constitution of a living system, because for anything to occur in a living system, it must undergo an actual ontogenic structural drift as an actual epigenic structural transformation that takes place in an actual history of interactions in the realization of a domain of existence. This is so even in the case of those particular ontogenic features or characters that we call genetically determined because they can be expected to appear in all the ontogenic drifts that a living system can possibly undergo up to the moment of its observation, because such a feature or character will appear only if there is an actual ontogeny. In these circumstances, a biological system of lineages, or system of phylogenies, is defined by the ontogenic phenotype conserved in the living systems which constitute it through their sequential reproductions. As a result, all the members of a system of lineages resemble each other through the ontogenic phenotype that defines the system of lineages, and not through a common genetic constitution maintained by means of a genetic flow.

7.10 Selection

An observer may claim that the actual ontogenic course followed by the structural changes of a living system is, moment by moment, selected by the medium from the many other ontogenic courses that he or she considers available to it at every instant during its life history. Yet, strictly speaking, selection does not take place in the life history of a living system. The life history of a living system is the particular course followed by its ontogenic drift under the contingencies of a particular sequence of interactions. As such, a life history is deterministically generated, instant after instant, as the structure of the living system changes through its own structurally determined dynamics in its continuous encounter with the medium as an independent entity, and lasts while the living system lasts. Each ontogeny, therefore, is uniquely generated as it takes place as a process that courses without actual alternatives or decision points along it.

The different ontogenic courses that an observer may describe as possible for a living system are alternative ontogenic courses only for her or him as she or he imagines the living system in different circumstances in the attempt to predict the one that will take place, while unable to compute by treating the living system and the medium as a known structure-determined system. The same is valid for the phylogenic structural drift, or for the historic genetic change in a population.

What an observer does when speaking of selection in relation to living systems, then, is to refer to a discrepancy between an expected and an actual historical outcome, and he or she does so by comparing the actual with the imagined in the phylogenic and the ontogenic structural drifts of living systems. Selection is not the mechanism that generates phylogenic structural change and adaptation. In fact, ontogenic and phylogenic structural changes and adaptation need not be explained, they are constitutive features of the condition of existence of living systems. All that has to be explained is the course followed by the continuous structural change that takes place in living systems, both in ontogeny and phylogeny, and this is explained by the mechanism of structural drift.

8. The answer

It follows from all that I have said about living systems that they exist only in conservation of organization and conservation of adaptation as constitutive conditions of their existence. This applies to the observer as a living system as well. It also follows that the present of any living system, the observer included is always that of a node in an ongoing network of co-phylogenic and co-ontogenic structural drifts. At the same time, as long as it is distinguished, any system is distinguished in conservation of organization and adaptation in its domain of existence, and a domain of existence is a domain of structural coupling that entails all the operational coherences that make possible the system that specifies it.

Let me summarize: first, every entity distinguished is distinguished in operational correspondence with its domain of existence, and therefore, each living system distinguished is necessarily distinguished in adequate action in its domain of structural coupling; second, an observer can only operate in adequate action in his or her domain of existence, and as such he or she does so as an expression of his or her conservation of organization and adaptation in it; third, an observer can only distinguish that which he or she distinguishes, and he or she does so as an expression of the operational coherences of the domain of praxis of living in which he or she makes the distinction. Let us now consider the question of cognition with all this in mind.

8.1 Cognition

Since the only criterion we have to assess cognition is to assess adequate action in a domain that we specify with a question, I proposed in *section 2* of this article that my task in explaining cognition as a biological phenomenon was to show how adequate action arises in any domain during the operation of a living system. This I have done by showing that a living system is necessarily always in adequate action in the domain in which it is distinguished as such in the praxis of living of the observer. This is so because it is constitutive of the phenomenon of observing that any system distinguished should be distinguished both in conservation of organization and structural coupling, and as a node in a network of structural drifts. In the distinction of living systems, this consists in bringing them forth in the praxis of living of the observer, both in conservation of autopoiesis and adaptation, and as a moment in their ontogenic drift in a medium, under conditions that constitute them in adequate action in their domains of existence.

In other words, I have shown that for any particular circumstance of distinction of a living system, conservation of living (conservation of autopoiesis and of adaptation) constitutes adequate action in those circumstances, and, hence, knowledge: *living systems are cognitive systems, and to live is to know*. But here, I have also shown that any interaction with a living system can be viewed by an observer as a question posed to it, as a challenge to its life that constitutes a domain of existence where he or she expects adequate action of it. At the same time, then, the actual acceptance by the observer of an answer to a question posed to a living system entails his or her recognition of adequate action by the living system in the domain specified by the question, and consists in the distinction of the latter in that domain under conditions of conservation of autopoiesis and adaptation. In what follows, I will present this general proposition in the guise of a particular scientific explanation.

a) The *phenomenon to be explained* is adequate action by a living system at any moment in which an observer distinguishes it as a living system in action in a particular domain. And I propose that on the understanding that the adequate actions of a living system are its interactions with conservation of class identity in the domain in which it is distinguished.

b) Given that structural coupling in its domain of existence (conservation of adaptation) is a condition of existence for any system distinguished by an observer, *the generative mechanism for adequate action* in a living system as a structurally changing system is the structural drift with conservation of adaptation through which it stays in continuous adequate action while it realizes its niche, or disintegrates. Since a system is distinguished only in structural coupling, when an observer distinguishes a living system, he or she necessarily distinguishes it as a system that constitutively remains in structural coupling in its domain of existence, regardless of how much its structure, or the structure of the medium, or both, change during the cause of his life.

c) Given the generative mechanism proposed in (b), it can be deduced that the following phenomena take place in the domain of experiences of an observer:
- the observer should see adequate action taking place in the form of co-ordinated behavior in living systems that are in co-ontogenic structural drift while in recurrent interactions with conservation of reciprocal adaptation;
- the observer should see that living systems in co-ontogeny should separate or disintegrate, or both, when their reciprocal adaptation is lost.

d) *The phenomena deduced in* (c) are apparent in the domain of experience of an observer in the dynamics of constitution and realization of a social system, and in all circumstances of recurrent interactions between living systems during their ontogenies, in what appears to us as learning to live together. One of these cases is our human operation in language.

The satisfaction of these four conditions results in: a) the validation, as a scientific explanation, of my proposition that cognition as adequate action in living systems is a consequence of their structural drift with conservation of organization and adaptation; b) the demonstration that adequate action (cognition) is constitutive to living systems because it is entailed in their existence as such; c) different living systems differing in their domains of adequate actions (domains of cognition) to the extent that they realize different niches; d) the domain of adequate actions (domain of cognition) of a living system changing like its own structure, or the structure of the medium, or both, changing while it conserves organization and adaptation.

At the same time it is apparent from all this, that what I say of cognition as an explanation of the praxis of living takes place in the praxis of living, and to the extent that what I say is effective action in the generation of the phenomenon of cognition, what I say takes place as cognition. If what I say sounds strange, it is only because we are in the habit of thinking about cognition with Objectivity without parentheses, as if the phenomenon connoted by the word cognition entailed pointing to something whose existence can be asserted to be independent of the pointing of the observer. I have shown that this is not and cannot be the case. Cognition cannot be understood as a biological phenomenon if objectivity is not put in parentheses, nor can it be understood as such if one is not willing to accept all the consequences of such an epistemological act.

Let us now consider human operation in language as one of the phenomena which take place as a consequence of the operation of cognition as adequate (or effective) action. This is particularly necessary because our operation in language, as observers in the praxis of living, is, at the same time, our problem and our instrument for analysis and explanation.

8.2 Language

We human beings are living systems that exist in language. This means that although we exist as human beings in language and our cognitive domains (domains of adequate actions) as such take place in the domain of languaging, our languaging takes place through our operation as living systems. Accordingly, that which I shall consider takes place in language as it arises as a biological phenomenon from the operation of living systems in recurrent interactions with conservation of organization and adaptation through their co-ontogenic structural drift, and thus show my object of consideration to be a consequence of the same mechanism that explains the phenomenon of cognition.

a) When two or more autopoietic systems interact recurrently, and in each of them a dynamic structure follows a course of change contingent upon the history of its interactions with the others, there is a co-ontogenic structural drift that gives rise to an ontogenically established domain of recurrent interactions between them, which appears to an observer as a domain of consensual coordinations of actions or distinctions in an environment. I call this ontogenically established domain of recurrent interactions a domain of consensual coordinations of actions or distinctions (a consensual domain of interactions), because it arises as a particular manner of living-together contingent upon the unique history or recurrent interactions of the participants during their co-ontogeny. Furthermore, because an observer can describe such a domain of recurrent interactions in semantic terms, by referring the different coordinations of actions (or distinctions) involved to the different consequences that they have in the domain in which they are distinguished, I also call a consensual domain of interactions a linguistic domain. Finally, I call the behavior through which an organism participates in an ontogenic domain of recurrent interactions consensual or linguistic, depending whether I want to emphasize the ontogenic origin of the behavior (consensual), or its implications in the present of the ongoing interactions (linguistic). Similarly, I speak of coordinations of actions or coordinations of distinctions, depending whether I want to emphasize what takes place in the interactions in relation to the participants (coordination of actions), or what takes place in the interactions in relation to an environment (coordinations of distinctions).

b) When one or more living systems continue their co-ontogenic structural drift through their recurrent interactions in a consensual domain, it is possible that a recursion takes place in their consensual behavior with the production of a consensual coordination of consensual coordinations of actions. An observer sees, when this happens, that the participants of a consensual domain of interactions operate in their consensual behavior, making consensual distinctions of their consensual distinctions, in a process that recursively makes a consensual action a consensual token for a consensual distinction that it obscures. Indeed, this is indistinguishable from that which takes place in our languaging in the praxis of living. Accordingly, I claim that the phenomenon of language takes place in the co-ontogeny of living systems when two or more organisms operate, through their recurrent ontogenic consensual interactions, in an ongoing process of recursive consensual coordinations of consensual coordinations of actions or distinctions (Maturana, 1978). Such recursive consensual coordination of consensual coordinations of actions or distinctions in any domain is the phenomenon of language. Furthermore, objects arise in language as consensual coordinations of actions, that operationally obscure for further recursive consensual coordinations of actions by the observers, the consensual coordinations of actions (distinctions) that they coordinate. Objects are in the process of languaging consensual coordinations of actions that operate as tokens for the consensual coordinations of actions that they coordinate. Objects do not pre-exist language. Finally, I claim that all the phenomena we as observers distinguish in our operation in language arise in the living of living systems, through their co-ontogenic structural drift, when this results in an ongoing process of consensual coordinations of actions, as a consequence of the proposed mechanism for the generation of the phenomenon of cognition.

c) Languaging takes place in the praxis of living: we human beings find ourselves as living systems immersed in it. In the explanation of language as a biological phenomenon, it becomes apparent that languaging arises, when it arises, as a manner of coexistence of living systems. As such, languaging takes place as a consequence of a co-ontogenic structural drift under recurrent consensual interactions. For this reason, language takes place as a system of recurrent interactions in a domain of structural coupling. Interactions in language do not take place in a domain of abstractions; on the contrary, they take place in the corporality of the participants. Interactions in language are structural interactions. Notions such as transmission of information, symbolization, denotation, meaning or syntax, are secondary to the constitution of the phenomenon of languaging in the living of the living systems that live it. Such notions arise as reflections in language upon that which takes place in languaging. It is for this reason that what takes place in language has consequences in our corporality, and the descriptions and explanations which we make become part of our domain of existence. We undergo our ontogenic and phylogenic drifts as human beings in structural coupling in our domain of existence as languaging systems. Language pertains to the praxis of living of observing, and generates the praxis of living of the observer.

9. Consequences

The answer given for this phenomenon of cognition has several fundamental consequences which I shall now consider.

9.1 Existence entails cognition

To the extent that cognition is the operation of a living system in its domain of structural coupling, i.e., in its domain of existence, existence of living systems entails cognition as their realization as such, not as a characterization or as a representation or as a disclosure of something independent of them. Cognition as a biological phenomenon takes place in a living system as it operates in its domain of perturbations, and as such it has no content and is not about anything. Therefore, when we say that we know *some-thing*, we are not connoting what happens in the mechanism of the phenomenon of cognition as a biological phenomenon, rather, we are reflecting in language upon what we do.

9.2 There are as many cognitive domains as there are domains of existence

I speak of cognition only in relation to living systems. This is arbitrary since what I have said in relation to existence applies to every entity brought forth through an operation of distinction. Therefore, I make this distinction only because I am speaking of living systems and the word cognition is historically bound to them through us. Notwithstanding this restriction, we as observers can say that there are as many domains of cognition as there are domains of existence specified by the different identities that living systems conserve through the realization of their autopoiesis. These different cognitive domains intersect in the structural realization of a living system, as this realizes the different identities that define them as different dimensions of simultaneous or successive structural couplings, orthogonal to the fundamental one in which the living system realizes its autopoiesis. As a result, these different cognitive domains may appear or disappear simultaneously or independently, according to whether the different structurally intersecting unities that specify them integrate or disintegrate independently or simultaneously (see *section 7.6*). Thus, when a student graduates, the cognitive domain specified by the operation in the domain of structural coupling that defines the identity *student* disappears together with the disintegration of the student. Or when a bachelor marries, the cognitive domain that the identity *bachelor* defines as a domain of operational coherences in structural coupling disappears, together with the disintegration of the bachelor. Conversely, when a student graduates and a bachelor marries, the identities *graduate* and *husband* appear with the corresponding cognitive domains specified by the operational coherences that they entail.

It follows from all this that a living system may operate in as many different cognitive domains as the different dimensions of its structural coupling allow it to realize. It also follows that the different identities that a living system may realize are necessarily fluid, and change as the dimensions on its structural coupling change with its structural drift in the happening of its living. To have an identity, to operate in a domain of cognition, is to operate in a domain of structural coupling.

9.3 Language is the human cognitive domain

Human beings as living systems operating in language operate in a domain of recursive reciprocal consensual perturbations that constitutes their domain of existence as such. Therefore, language as a domain of recursive consensual coordinations of actions is a domain of existence, and as such a cognitive domain defined by the recursion of consensual distinctions in a domain of consensual distinctions. Furthermore, human beings as living systems operating in language constitute observation, and become observers, by bringing forth objects as primary consensual coordinations of actions in a process that obscures the actions which they coordinate. Human beings, therefore, exist in the domain of objects that they bring forth through languaging. At the same time, human beings, by existing as observers in the domain of objects brought forth through languaging, exist in a domain that allows them to explain the happening of their living in language through reference to their operation in a domain of dynamic reciprocal structural coupling.

9.4 Objectivity

Objects arise in language as consensual coordinations of actions that, in a domain of consensual distinctions, are tokens for more basic coordinations of actions that they obscure. Without language and outside language, there are no objects because objects are only constituted as consensual coordinations of actions in the recursion of consensual coordinations of actions that languaging is. There are no objects for living systems that do not operate in language; for them, objects are not part of their cognitive domains. Since we human beings are objects in a domain of objects that we bring forth and handle in language, language is our peculiar domain of existence and peculiar cognitive domain. In these circumstances, objectivity arises in language as a manner of operating with objects without distinguishing the actions that they obscure. In this operation, descriptions arise as concatenations of consensual coordinations of actions that result in further consensual coordinations of actions which, if elaborated without distinction as to how objects arise, can be distinguished as manners of languaging that take place as if objects existed outside of language. Objects are operational relations in languaging.

9.5 Languaging: operation in a domain of structural coupling

To the extent that language arises as a consensual domain in the co-ontogenic structural drift of living systems involved in recurrent interactions, organisms that operate in language operate in a domain of reciprocal co-ontogenic structural coupling through reciprocal structural perturbations. Therefore, to operate in language is not an *abstract* activity as we usually think. To language is to interact structurally. Language takes place in the domain of relations between organisms in the recursion of consensual coordinations of consensual actions, but at the same time, language takes place through structural interactions in the domain of the corporality of the languaging organisms. In other words, although languaging takes place in the social domain as a dance of recursive relations of coordinations of actions, interactions in language as structural interactions are orthogonal to that domain, and as such trigger in the corporality of the participants structural changes that change the physiological background (emotional standing) on which they continue their languaging as much the course that this takes. The result is that the social coordinations of actions of languaging, as elements of a domain of recursive operation in structural coupling, become part of the medium in which the participating living systems conserve organization and adaptation through the structural changes that they undergo contingent to their participation in that domain. Thus, although the domain of coordinations of actions and the domain of structural change of the participants in language do not intersect, their changes are coupled orthogonally through the structural interactions that take place in language. As the body changes, languaging changes, and as languaging changes the body changes. Here resides the power of words. Words are abstract entities in languaging and structural interactions in language, and it is through this that the world we bring forth in languaging becomes part of the domain in which our ontogenic and phylogenic structural drifts take place.

9.6 Language is a domain of descriptions

Language is a system of recursive consensual coordinations of actions in which every consensual coordination of actions becomes an object through a recursion in the consensual coordinations of actions, in a process that becomes the operation of distinction that distinguishes it and constitutes the observer. In these circumstances, all participants in a language domain can be observers with respect to the sequences of coordinations of actions in which they participate, constituting a system of recursive distinctions in which systems of distinctions become objects of distinctions. Such recursive distinctions of distinctions in the happening of living in language, which bring forth systems of objects, constitute the phenomenon of description. As a result, all that there is in the human domain are descriptions in the happening of living in language which become objects of descriptions in language. Descriptions, however, do not replace the happening of living that they constitute as descriptions, they only expand it in recursions which follow its operational coherences. Accordingly, scientific explanations, as systems of descriptions, do not replace the phenomena that they explain in the domain of happening of living of the observer, but bring forth operational coherences in that domain, which allow for further descriptions in it.

9.7 Self-consciousness arises with language

For a living system in its operation as a closed system there is no inside or outside, it has no way of making the distinction. Yet in language, such a distinction arises as a particular consensual coordination of actions in which the participants are recursively brought forth as distinctions of systems of distinctions. When this happens, self-consciousness arises as a domain of distinctions in which the observers participate in the consensual distinctions of their participations in language through languaging. It follows from this that the individual exists only in language, that the self exists only in language, and that self-consciousness as a phenomenon of self distinctions takes place only in language. Furthermore, since language as a domain of consensual coordinations of actions is a social phenomenon, self-consciousness is a social phenomenon, and as such it does not take place within the anatomical confines of the corporality of the living systems that generate it. On the contrary, it is external to them and pertains to their domain of interactions as a manner of co-existence.

9.8 History

The significance or meaning of any given behavior resides in the circumstances of its enaction, not in the characteristics of the dynamics of states of the behaving living system or in any particular feature of the behavior itself. In other words, it is not the complexity of the inner states of a living system or of its nervous system, nor any aspect of the behavior itself, which determines the nature, meaning, relevance or content of any given behavior, but its placement in the ongoing historical process in which it arises. The higher human functions do not take place in the brain: language, abstract thinking, love, devotion, reflection, rationality, altruism, etc. are not features of the dynamics of states of the human being as a living system, nor of its nervous system as a neuronal network, they are socio-historical phenomena. At the same time, history is not part of the dynamics of states of a living system because this takes place only in the present, instant after instant in the operation of its structure in changes that occur out of time. History, time, future, past or space, exist in language as forms of explaining the happening of living of the observer, and thereby partake of the involvement of language in this. Therefore, it is in the explanation of the happening of living through the coherences of language that an observer can claim that the structure of a living system that determines its changes of state in the present always embodies its history of interactions, because it continuously arises in the present in a structural drift contingent to such a history.

9.9 The nervous system expands the domain of states of the living system

For living systems to operate in language the diversity and plasticity of their internal states must match the diversity of the changing circumstances generated in their recursive consensual coordinations of actions. In other words, although language does not take place within the bodyhood of the living system, the structure of the living system must provide the diversity and plasticity of states required for it to take place. The nervous system participates in this by expanding the domain of states of the organism through the richness and recursiveness of its dynamics as a closed network of changing relations of neuronal activities (Maturana 1983), and by expanding in the organism the domain of its changes of states, which follow in it a course contingent upon both, upon its own changes of states and upon its interactions in the medium. This nervous system does so: a) by admitting the interactions of the organism as orthogonal perturbations from the medium, which is a condition that makes its structural drift as a cellular network (as well as the structural drift of the organism and its participation in the generation of behavior), contingent upon the history of those interactions; and b) by admitting orthogonal interactions from the components of the organism, a condition that makes its structural drift as a cellular network, as well as the structural drift of the organism and its participation in the generation of behavior, recursively contingent upon the dynamics of structural changes of the organism. The result of all this for the organism (including its nervous system) is the possibility of the recursive involvement of its dynamics of states with the ongoing flow of its own dynamics of states through its behavior, if it has sufficient plasticity in the nervous system and participates in a sufficiently large domain of recurrent interactions with other organisms. Indeed, this is what permits the production of language, as this arises when the internal recursiveness of the dynamics of states of the nervous system couples with the recurrence of social consensual coordinations of actions, giving rise to the recursion of consensual coordinations as an ongoing process in the generation of social behavior.

The ongoing recursive coupling of behavioral and structural changes that give origin to language is possible because a structure-determined system exists in two non-intersecting phenomenal domains realized through orthogonally dependent structures, namely, its domain of states and its domain of interactions. It is our basic double existence as structure-determined systems in two non-intersecting but orthogonally coupled phenomenal domains, which permits us in our operation in language to generate endless orthogonally interdependent and yet non-intersecting phenomenal domains in the happening of our living.

9.10 Observing takes place in languaging

The nervous system is a closed network of interacting active neuronal elements (neurons, effectors and receptors) that are structurally realized as cellular components of the organism. As such it operates as a closed network of changing relations of activity between its components: it is constitutive to the organization of the nervous system that any change of relations of activity between its components should lead to further changes of relations of activity between them, and that in this sense it should operate without inputs or outputs. Therefore, any action upon an environment that an observer sees as a result of the operation of the nervous system, is a feature of the structural changes that take place in it as a cellular network (muscular contraction, glandular secretion), and not as a feature of its operation as such. Indeed, the operation of the nervous system and the actions of the organism take place in non-intersecting phenomenal domains realized by orthogonally related structures.

Similarly, any perturbation of the medium impinging upon the organism is a perturbation in the structure of the nervous system, not an input in its dynamics of states. If this changes, it does so because the structure of the nervous system changes in a manner contingent to perturbation, not because it admits an input to operation. As a result of all this, all that takes place in the nervous system is a dance of changing relations of neuronal activities, which in the domain of structural coupling where the observer beholds the organism appears as a dance of changing configurations of effector/sensor correlations. An observer who sees an effector/sensor correlation as adequate behavior does so because he or she beholds the organism in the domain of structural coupling in which the behavior distinguished takes place in the flow of its conservation of adaptation. The organism in its operation does not act upon an environment, nor does the nervous system operate with a representation of one in the generation of the adequate behavior of the organism. The environment exists only for an observer, and as such it is a phenomenon of languaging.

That the nervous system should operate as a closed network of changing relations of activity between its components, and not with representations of an environment has two fundamental consequences:

a) For the operation of the nervous system, everything is the same. All that takes place in the operation of the nervous system are changes of relations of activity between its components, and it does not distinguish in its operation whether its changes of state arise through its internal dynamics or as a result of structural changes triggered in it through that which an observer sees as external structural perturbations.

b) For the observer, the organism operates in many different domains of structural coupling which intersect operationally in the domain of states of the nervous system through the structural perturbations generated in it by the interactions of the organism in these different domains. As a result of this several things happen that are relevant for the understanding of the domains of reality that the observer brings forth. Firstly, an observer can always treat a state of activity of the nervous system (a configuration of changes of relations of activity) that arises as a result of a particular interaction of the organism, as a representation of that interaction, and he or she can do so by constituting the domain of descriptions as a meta-phenomenal domain in which both are distinguished together. Secondly, different states of activity of the nervous system, which for an observer represent interactions of the organism in non-intersecting phenomenal domains (different domains of structural coupling), can affect each other and give rise to behaviors of the organism that constitute meta-domains of relations between the phenomena that take place in those non-intersecting phenomenal domains. Thirdly, the meta-domains of relations, established through their operational intersection in the domain of states of the nervous system by the operation of the organism in its different domains of structural coupling constitute, through the behaviors that these intersections generate, new domains of structural coupling of the organism that do not intersect with the others. Fourthly, the operational intersection of the different domains of interactions (different domains of structural coupling) of an organism in the operation of its nervous system allows it to operate in recurrent interactions with other organisms in the continuous recursive generation of meta-domains of relations which become phenomenal domains in their own right in the ongoing flow of those recurrent interactions.

The result of all this is the possibility of the constitution of the observer, when two or more organisms generate observing in their recursive consensual coordinations of actions, as they operate in reciprocal references for the constitution of meta domains of relations in their ongoing recurrent interactions. As a result of this, the activity of observing also becomes an operation in language with operational coherences brought forth in language. Since the operation of the nervous system appears in the domain of operation of the organism as sensory/effector correlations, observing signifies coordinations of the corporality of observers through their generation of a choreography of interlaced sensory/effector correlations. In fact, all that there is for the operation of the nervous system of the observer in observing is its closed dynamics of changing relations between its neuronal components. It is only for an observer who sees two or more interacting organisms in his or her praxis of living, that the sensory/effector correlations of these appear recursively involved with each other in a network of recursive sensory/effector correlations constituted through the orthogonal interactions of their nervous systems. Finally, it is only for an observer that such a network of recursive sensory/effector correlations becomes language, and a meta-domain with respect to the operation of the nervous system where explanations and observing takes place, when it becomes a recursive system of consensual coordinations of consensual actions.

10. The domain of physical existence

A domain of existence is a domain of operational coherences entailed by the distinction of a unity by an observer in his or her praxis of living. As such, a domain of existence arises as the domain of the operational validity of the properties of the unity distinguished, if it is a simple unity, or as the domain of validity of the properties of the components of the unity distinguished, if this is a composite one. As a consequence, the distinction of a unity entails its domain of existence as a composite unity that includes it as a component. There are, therefore, as many domains of existence as kinds of unities an observer may bring forth in his or her operations of distinction. In these circumstances, since the notion of determinism applies to the operation of the properties of the components of a unity in its composition all domains of existence, as composite entities that include the unities that specify them, conform to deterministic systems in the sense indicated above. This has certain consequences for us living systems existing in language, and for the explanations that we generate as such.

a) Our domain of existence as the composite unities that we are, as molecular autopoietic systems is the domain of existence of our component molecules, and entails all the operational coherences proper to the molecular existence. Therefore, our existence as autopoietic systems implies the satisfaction of all the constraints that the distinction of molecules entails, and our operation as molecular systems implies the determinism entailed in the distinction of molecules.

b) If we distinguish molecules as composite entities, they exist in the domain of existence of their components, and as such, their existence implies the satisfaction of the determinism that the distinction of the latter entails. The same applies to the decomposition of the components of molecules, and so on, recursively. Since unities and their domains of existence are brought forth and specified in their distinction in the happening of living of the observer, the only limit to the recursion in distinctions is the limit of the diversity of experiences of the observer in his or her happening of living (praxis).

c) Since the observer as a living system is a composite entity, the observer makes distinctions in his or her interactions as a living system through the operation of the properties of his or her components. If the observer uses an instrument, then his or her distinctions take place through the operation of the properties of the instrument as if this were one of its components. The result of this is that an observer cannot make distinctions outside of her or his domain of existence as a composite entity.

d) Descriptions are series of consensual distinctions subject to recursive consensual distinctions in a community of observers. Observers operate in language only through their recursive interactions in the domain of structural coupling, in which they recursively coordinate consensual actions as operations in their domains of experiences through the praxis of their living. Therefore, all interactions in language between observers take place through the operation of the properties of their components as living systems in the domain of their reciprocal structural coupling. We as human beings operate in language only through our interactions in our domain of existence as living systems, and we cannot make descriptions that entail interactions outside this domain. As a consequence, although language as a domain of recursive consensual distinctions is open to unending recursions, language is a closed operational domain in the sense that it is not possible to step outside language through language, and descriptions cannot be characterizations of independent entities.

e) Since everything said is said by an observer to another observer, and since objects (entities, things) arise in language, we cannot operate with objects (entities or things) as if they existed outside the distinctions of distinctions that constitute them. Furthermore, as entities in language, objects are brought forth as explanatory elements in the explanation of the operational coherences of the happening of living in which languaging takes place. Without observers nothing exists, and with observers everything that exists exists in explanation.

f) As we put objectivity in parentheses because we recognize that we cannot experientially distinguish between what we commonly call perception and illusion, we accept that existence is specified by an operation of distinction. Nothing exists prior to its distinction. In this sense, houses, persons, atoms or elementary particles are not different. Also in this sense, existence as an explanation of the praxis of living of the observer is a cognitive phenomenon that reflects the ontology of observing in such a praxis of living. It is not a claim about objectivity. Therefore, with objectivity in parentheses, an entity has no continuity beyond or outside that specified by the coherences which constitute its domain of existence, as this is brought forth in its distinction. The claims that the house to which I return every evening from work is the same that I left in the morning, or that whenever I see my mother I see the same person who gave birth to me, or that all the points of the path of an electron in a bubble chamber are traces left by the same electron, are claims that constitute cognitive statements, which define sameness in the distinction of the unity (house, mother, or electron), as this is specified in the operation of distinction that brings it forth together with its domain of existence. Since cognitive statements are not and cannot be statements about the properties of independent objects, sameness is necessarily always a reflection of the observer in observing in the domain of existence that he or she brings forth in his or her distinctions. Furthermore, since no entity can be distinguished outside its domain of existence as the domain of operational coherences in which it is possible, every distinction specifies a domain of existence as a domain of possible distinctions. Every distinction specifies a domain of existence as a versum in the multiversa, every distinction specifies a domain of reality.

g) A scientific explanation entails the proposition of a mechanism (or composite entity) that, if realized, would generate the phenomenon to be explained in the domain of experiences (praxis or happening of living) of the observer (*section 4*). The generative character of the scientific explanation is constitutive to it. Indeed, this ontological condition in science carries with it the legitimacy of the foundational character of the phenomenal domain in which the generative explanatory mechanism takes place, as well as the legitimacy of treating every entity distinguished as a composite unity, by asking for the origin of its properties in its organization and structure. And because this is also the case for our commonsense explanations in our effective operation in daily life, it seems natural to us to ask for a substratum independent of the observer as the ultimate medium in which everything takes place. Yet, although it is an epistemological necessity to expect such a substratum, we constitutively cannot assert its existence by distinguishing it as a composite entity and characterizing it in terms of components and relations between components. In order to do so we would have to describe it, that is, we would have to bring it forth in language and give it form in the domain of recursive consensual coordinations of actions in which we exist as human beings. However, to do so would be tantamount to characterizing the substratum in terms of entities (things, properties) that arise through languaging, and which, as consensual distinctions of consensual coordinations of actions, are constitutively not the substratum. Through language we remain in language, and we lose the substratum as soon as we attempt to language it. We need the substratum for epistemological reasons, but in the substratum there are no objects, entities or properties. In the substratum there is nothing (no-thing) because things belong to language. Nothing exists in the substratum.

h) Distinctions take place in the domain of experiences, in the happening or praxis of living of the observer as a human being. For this reason, the domain of operational coherences which an observer brings forth in the distinction of a unity as its domain of existence, also occurs in his or her domain of experiences as a human being as part of his or her praxis of living. Therefore, since language is operation in a domain of recursive consensual co-ordinations of consensual actions in the domain of experiences of the observers as human beings, all dimensions of the domains of experiences of the observers exist in language as co-ordinations of actions between observers. As such, all descriptions constitute configurations of coordinations of actions in some dimensions of the domains of experiences of the members of a community of observers in co-ontogenic structural drift. Physics, biology, mathematics, philosophy, cooking, politics, etc. are all different domains of languaging, and as such, are all different domains of recursive consensual coordinations of consensual actions in the praxis or happening of living of the members of a community of observers. It is only as different domains of languaging that physics, biology, philosophy, cooking, politics, or any cognitive domain, exist. Yet this does not mean that all cognitive domains are the same, it only means that different cognitive domains exist only as they are brought forth in language, and that languaging constitutes them.

We talk as if things existed in the absence of the observer, as if the domain of operational coherences which we bring forth in a distinction would operate as it operates in our distinctions regardless of them. We now know that this is constitutively not the case. We talk, for example, as if time and matter were independent dimensions of the physical space. Yet, it is apparent from my explanation of the phenomenon of cognition that they are not and cannot be. Indeed, time and matter are explanations of some of the operational coherences of the domains of existence brought forth in the distinctions that constitute the ongoing languaging of the praxis of living of the members of a community of observers. Thus, time, with past, present and future arises as a feature of an explanatory mechanism that would generate what an observer experiences as mutually impenetrable simultaneous distinctions. Without observers, nothing can be said, explained, or claimed. In fact, without observers, nothing exists because existence is specified in the operation of distinction of the observer. For epistemological reasons, we ask for a substratum that could provide an independent ultimate justification or validation of distinguishability. However, for ontological reasons, such a substratum remains beyond our reach as observers. All that we can say ontologically about the substratum is that it permits all the operational coherences which we bring forth in the happening of living as we exist in language.

As we operate in language, we operate in a domain of reciprocal structural coupling in our domain of existence as composite unities (molecular autopoietic systems); that is, we operate in the domain of existence of our components. Therefore, anything that we say, any explanation that we propose, can only entail distinctions that involve the operation of our components in their domain of existence as we operate as observers in language. Accordingly, it is in the domain where we exist as composite entities, the domain where we distinguish molecules, atoms or elementary particles as entities, that we bring forth in language operations of distinction which specify them and the operational coherences of their domains of existence. If what we call the physical domain of existence is the domain where physicists distinguish molecules, atoms or elementary particles, then we as living systems specify the domain of physical existence as our limiting cognitive domain as we operate as observers in language, interacting in the domain of existence of our components as we bring it forth as an explanation of the happening of our living. We do not exist in a pre-existing domain of physical existence, we bring it forth and specify it as we exist as observers. The experience of the physicist, should it be in classic, relativistic or quantum physics, does not reflect the nature of *the universe*, it reflects the ontology of the observer as a living system as he or she operates in language bringing forth the physical entities and the operational coherences of their domains of existence.

As Einstein asserted "scientific theories (explanations) are free creations of the human mind." Then, in a seeming paradox, he asked the question, "how is it, if that is the case, that the universe is intelligible through them?"

In this article I have shown that there is no paradox if one reveals the ontology of observing and the ontology of scientific explanations by putting objectivity in parentheses. Indeed, I have shown that a scientific explanation entails: a) the proposition of a phenomenon to be explained, brought forth as such *a priori* in the praxis of living of the observer; b) the proposition of an *ad hoc* generative mechanism, also brought forth *a priori* in the praxis of living of the observer, which if allowed to operate would generate the phenomenon being explained as a consequence to be witnessed by the observer in her or his praxis of living; c) the operational coherence of the four operational conditions constituting its criterion of validation, as they are realized in the praxis of living of the observer; d) the superfluousness and impertinence of the assumption of objectivity. From all this, it follows that the explanatory mechanism proposed in a scientific explanation is constitutively "a free creation of the human mind," because it is brought forth constitutively *a priori* in the praxis of living of the observer, which is without any justification other than the *ad hoc* generative character of the phenomenon explained. Accordingly, a scientific explanation constitutively explains the universe (versum) in which it takes place, because both the explanatory mechanism and the phenomenon being explained occur in a generative relation, as non-intersecting phenomena of the same operational domain of the praxis of living of the observer. Since the operation of distinction specifies the entity distinguished as well as its domain of existence, a scientific explanation constitutively explains the universe (versum) in which it takes place because it brings with it the domain of operational coherences (the versum of the multiversa) of the praxis of living of the observer which it makes intelligible. Strictly speaking then, there is no paradox: scientific explanations do not explain an independent world or universe, they explain the praxis of living (the domain of experiences) of the observer, making use of the same operational coherences that constitute it in languaging. It is here where science becomes poetry.

11. Reality

The word reality comes from the latin noun *res,* meaning object (thing), and it is commonly used to signify objectivity without parentheses. The real, and sometimes the really real, is meant to be that which exists independently of the observer. We know now that the concepts engendered by this way of speaking havve no foundation. Objects, things, arise in language when a consensual coordination of actions, by being consensually distinguished in a recursion of consensual coordinations of actions, obscures the actions that it coordinates in the praxis of living in a consensual domain. An object is brought forth in language in an operation of distinction which is a configuration of consensual coordinations of actions. When an object is distinguished in language, its domain of existence as a coherent domain of consensual coordinations of actions becomes a domain of objects, a domain of reality, a versum of the multiversa, so that all that it entails, is all that is entailed in the consensual coordinations of actions that constitute it. Every domain of existence is a domain of reality, and all domains of reality are equally valid domains of existence brought forth by an observer as domains of coherent consensual actions that specify all that there is in them. Once a domain of reality is brought forth, the observer can treat the objects or entities that constitute it as if they were all that there is and as if they existed independently of the operations of distinction that bring them forth. And this is so because a domain of reality is brought forth in the praxis of living of the observer as a domain of operational coherences which requires no internal justification.

Therefore, an observer operating in a domain of reality necessarily operates in a domain of effective actions. Another observer may claim that the first one errs or has an illusion only when this begins to operate in a domain of reality different from the one that he or she expected. If we specify an operation of distinction, *ghost*, then ghosts exist, are real in the domain of existence brought forth in their distinction and we can act effectively with them in that domain, but they are not real in any other domain. Indeed, everything is an illusion outside its domain of existence. Every domain of reality, as a domain of operational coherences brought forth in the happening of living of the observer in language, is a closed domain of effective consensual actions, i.e., a cognitive domain. Conversely, every cognitive domain as a domain of operational coherences is a domain of reality.

What is uncanny, perhaps, is that although different domains of reality are seen by an observer as different domains of coordinations of actions in an environment, they are lived by the observer as different domains of languaging which differ only through their ongoing transformation in the different circumstances of recursion in which they arise. We as observers can now explain this as follows: as we operate in language through our consensual interactions in the happening of living of a community of observers, our structural drift in the happening of our living becomes contingent upon the course of those consensual interactions. And this takes place in a manner which keeps the transformation of the happening of our living congruent with the domain of reality that we bring forth in that community of observers, or else we disintegrate as members of it. It is this which makes us observing systems, capable through language of an endless recursive generation of new cognitive domains (new domains of reality) as new domains of praxes of observing in our continuous structural drifts as living systems.

12. Self-consciousness and reality

The self arises in language in the linguistic recursion that brings forth the observer as an entity in the explanation of his or her operation in a domain of consensual distinctions. Self-consciousness arises in language in the linguistic recursion that brings forth the distinction of the self as an entity in the explanation of the operation of the observer in the distinction of the self from other entities in a consensual domain of distinctions. As a result, reality arises with self-consciousness in language as an explanation of the distinction between self and non-self in the praxis of living of the observer. Self, self-consciousness and reality exist in language as explanations of the happening of living of the observer. Indeed, the observer as human being in language is primary with respect to self and self-consciousness, and these arise as he or she operates in language, explaining his or her praxis of living as such. That the entities brought forth in our explanations should have an unavoidable presence in our domain of existence is because we are realized as observers, as we distinguish them in the domain of operational coherences that they define as we distinguish them. We do not go through a wall in the praxis of living because we exist as living systems in the same domain of operational coherences in which a wall exists as a molecular entity, and a wall is distinguished as a composite entity in the molecular space as that entity through which we cannot go as molecular entities.

The observer is primary, not the object. Observing is given in the praxis of living in language, and we are already in it when we begin to reflect upon it. Matter, energy, ideas, notions, mind, spirit, god, etc. are explanatory propositions of the praxis of living of the observer. Furthermore, as explanatory propositions, they entail different manners of living of the observer in recursive conservation of adaptation in the domains of operational coherences brought forth in their different distinctions. Thus, when the observer operates within an objectivity without parentheses, he or she operates in an explanatory avenue which neglects the experiential indistinguishability between what we call perception and illusion. Yet when he or she operates within an objectivity in parentheses, he or she operates in an explanatory avenue which accepts this indistinguishability as a starting point. In the explanatory path of objectivity without parentheses, neither observer, nor language nor perception can be explained scientifically because a contradiction arises with the structural determinism of the living system. Whereas within an objectivity in parentheses there is no such contradiction.

As one operates within any given domain of reality, one can operate within an objectivity without parentheses without contradiction. But when a disagreement arises with another observer, and one thinks that it is not a matter of a simple logical mistake, one is forced to claim a privileged access to an objective reality to resolve it and to deal with errors as if they were *mistaking* of what is. If in similar circumstances one is operating within an objectivity in parentheses, one finds that the disagreeing parties operate in different domains of reality, and that the disagreement disappears only when they begin to operate in the same one. Furthermore, one also finds that errors are changes of domains of reality in the operation of an observer which he or she notices only *a posteriori*. Finally, by operating within an objectivity without parentheses, we cannot explain how an observer operates in the generation of a scientific explanation because we take for granted the abilities of the observer. Contrary to this, as we operate within an objectivity in parentheses, scientific explanations and the observer appear as components in a single closed generative explanatory mechanism, in which the properties or abilities of the observer are shown to arise in a phenomenal domain other than the one in which its components operate.

We human beings exist only as we exist as self-conscious entities in language. It is only as we exist as self-conscious entities that the domain of physical existence exists as our limiting cognitive domain in the ultimate explanation of the human observer's happening of living. The physical domain of existence is secondary to the happening of living of the human observer, even though in the explanation of observing, the human observer arises from the physical domain of existence. Indeed, the understanding of the ontological primacy of observing is basic for the understanding of the phenomenon of cognition. Human existence is a cognitive existence and takes place through languaging, yet cognition has no content and does not exist outside the effective actions that constitute it.

This is why nothing exists outside the distinctions of the observer. That the physical domain of existence should be our limiting cognitive domain does not alter this. Nature, the world, society, science, religion, the physical space, atoms, molecules, trees, etc., indeed all things, are cognitive entities, explanations of the praxis or happening of living of the observer. And as this very explanation, they only exist as a bubble of human actions floating on nothing. Everything is cognitive, and the bubble of human cognition changes in the continuous happening of the human recursive involvement in co-ontogenic and co-phylogenic drifts with the domains of existence that he or she brings forth in the praxis of living. Everything is human responsibility.

The atom and the hydrogen bombs are cognitive entities. The big bang, or whatever we claim from our present praxis of living to have given origin to the physical versum, is a cognitive entity, an explanation of the praxis of living of the observer bound to the ontology of observing. That is their reality. Our happening of living takes place regardless of our explanations, but its course becomes contingent upon our explanations as they become part of the domain of existence in which we conserve organization and adaptation through our structural drifts. Our living takes place in structural coupling with the world which we bring forth, and the world which we bring forth is our doing as observers in language, as we operate in structural coupling in it in the praxis of living. We cannot do anything outside our domains of structural coupling: we cannot do anything outside our domains of cognition. This is why nothing that we do as human beings is trivial, and everything that we do becomes part of the world as we bring it forth as social entities in language. Human responsibility in the multiversa is total.

ONTOLOGY OF OBSERVING

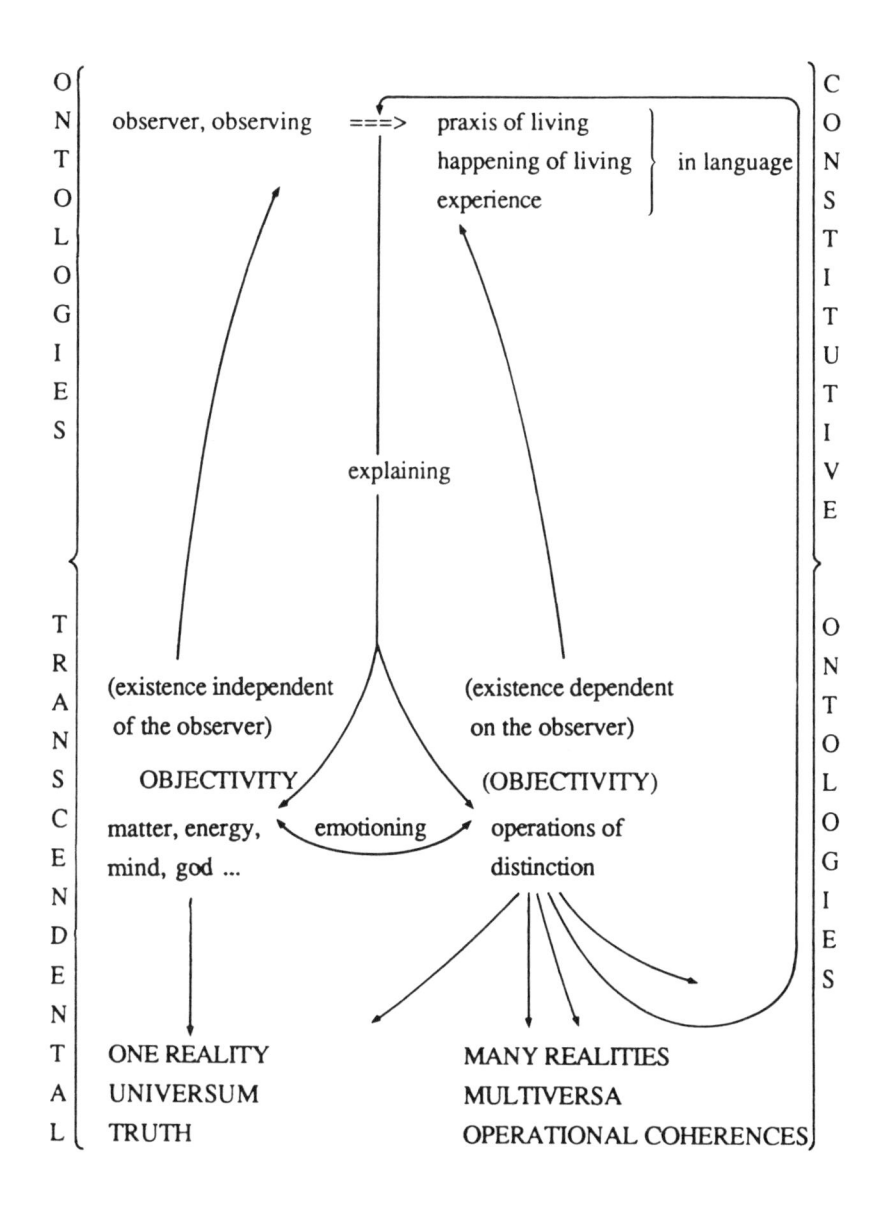

```
ONTOLOGIES {                                                                          } CONSTITUTIVE
              observer, observing ===> praxis of living    ⎫
                                       happening of living ⎬ in language
                                       experience          ⎭

                              explaining

TRANSCENDENTAL {                                                                      } ONTOLOGIES
              (existence independent         (existence dependent
               of the observer)               on the observer)

              OBJECTIVITY                    (OBJECTIVITY)
              matter, energy,  emotioning   operations of
              mind, god ...                  distinction

              ONE REALITY                    MANY REALITIES
              UNIVERSUM                      MULTIVERSA
              TRUTH                          OPERATIONAL COHERENCES
```

Niklas Luhmann

Sthenographie

I

Es ist kein Druckfehler, um das vorab klarzustellen. Es soll nicht von Kurzschrift die Rede sein. Stheno ist eine der Gorgonen, deren Anblick jeden Sterblichen erstarren läßt. Es handelt sich, man wird sich erinnern, um drei Schwestern. Nur eine von ihnen ist sterblich: Medusa. Sie kann getötet werden. Stheno dagegen, nebst Euryale, ist unsterblich. Man muß sich also nicht nur bei einem Versuch, sie zu töten, vorsehen, sondern hat gar keine andere Wahl als: nicht hinzuschauen.

Den Anlaß, an die Gorgonen zu erinnern, bietet eine neuere Diskussion über Paradoxien. Einerseits gibt es seit Frege und Russell die Bemühungen, Paradoxien aus der Konstruktion formaler Systeme zu eliminieren. Das hat zu der Ansicht geführt, es handele sich um Sonderprobleme, um versteckte Fehler gleichsam, die man aufspüren und ausmerzen müsse. Man nimmt sich, wie Perseus, die Medusa vor; oder man versucht, ein abgegrenztes Feld unter Kultur zu halten und gar nicht erst in die Wildnis auszuziehen. Ein echter, an Welt und damit an sich selbst interessierter Philosoph ist mit diesen Auswegen jedoch nie zufrieden gewesen. Er sieht Paradoxieprobleme, heute mehr denn je, als eine Herausforderung an die Rationalität seiner Konstruktionen. Manchmal, ich zitiere MacKie, hat er noch den Mut, "to look them calmly in the face when he encounters them in the wilderness where they are at home."[1] Lebensmut oder Sterbensmut - jedenfalls verläßt diese Art Philosophen sich zumeist auf eine vermeintlich zahlungsfähige Versicherung, auf die Ontologie und ihren Wahrheitsbegriff.[2] Das erlaubt es ihnen, anstelle der Gorgonen einfach eine Leere zu sehen, eine Position ohne Inhalt. Paradoxien sind dann Formulierungen, die nichts besagen, weil ihnen nichts entspricht. Die logischen oder rhetorischen Künste, mit denen sie konstruiert werden, beweisen nur, daß man ohne einen ontologischen Wahrheitsbegriff nicht zurechtkommt. Aber sehen diese Philosophen richtig hin? Und sehen sie die Leere, das Schweigen, die Weiße des Papiers als unerläßliche Bedingung für Differenz, für Übergänge, für Fortsetzbarkeit autopoietischer Operationen, für Formbildung, für Systembildung?[3] Über Nietzsche und Heidegger bis zu Derrida hat sich inzwischen ein ganz anderer Umgang mit Paradoxien eingebürgert. Hilary Lawson[4] hat darin geradezu die Philosophie dieses Jahrhunderts gesehen. Die Paradoxien werden nicht vermieden oder umgangen, sondern vorgeführt. Sie werden mit Hingebung zelebriert. Sie werden in einer wie immer verdrehten Sprache zum Ausdruck gebracht. Fast glaubt man, die Absicht zu erkennen, die Gorgonen wie einen Schild zu benutzen, sie vor sich herzutragen, um andere damit zu erschrecken. Erst dies ist nun eigentlich Sthenographie. Es ist zur Zeit nicht leicht, ein Urteil zu fällen. Beeindruckt ist man zunächst durch die Radikalität, mit der die traditionellen Denkweisen Europas verabschiedet und daraus die Konsequenzen gezogen werden. Auch als Soziologe würde man ja meinen, daß die moderne Gesellschaft ein historisch unvergleichbarer Sonderfall ist, der alle gewohnten Beschreibungsmittel obsolet werden läßt. Die Vermutung spricht für Diskontinuität - in der Sozialstruktur ebenso wie in der Semantik. Andererseits hat die neue Sthenographie bisher noch nicht viel erbracht. Die Paradoxierung der Zivilisation hat nicht zur Zivilisierung des Paradoxen geführt. Auch fragt man sich, ob es angemessen wäre, die höchst dynamische Gesellschaft mit einer Semantik zu beschreiben, die auf eine Mixtur von Beliebigkeit und Lähmung hinausläuft. Tatsächlich sind ja deutlich gerichtete (keineswegs beliebige) Trends zu beobachten und nicht frei erfundene Variationen, sondern Engpässe, Risiken und Gefahren, auf die das ganze Menschheitsunternehmen Sinn zuzulaufen scheint. Im übrigen scheint die Sthenographie hauptsächlich Literaten und, in gewissem Umfange, Philosophieexperten zu beeindrucken, und Beobachter der Szene können bereits die für Gorgonenbetrachter voraussagbare Erstarrung feststellen. Das kommt davon!

Dies ist jedoch nicht alles. Auch ganz andere Quellen motivieren heute zur Beschäftigung mit Paradoxien. Wenn man die bisher sichtbaren, sehr heterogenen Ansätze vergleichend betrachtet, gewinnt man den Eindruck, Paradoxien hätten eine zur Kreativität anreizende Funktion. Die Sthenographen gehen davon aus, daß ein logisch einwandfreier Begriff der Paradoxie nicht gewonnen werden kann, weil die Logik selbst ja ein paradoxiefreies Kalkül zu sein beansprucht. Die Logik verwendet Paradoxien zur Markierung eines logisch kontrollierbaren Raums. Für sie sind Paradoxien Grenzmarken, die sie aber nur von innen und nicht von außen, nur als Bedingung der Möglichkeit ihrer eigenen Operationen, aber nicht als Form sehen kann.[5] Die Logik kann nur so viel sehen, daß Aussagen, auf deren Wahrheit sie nicht verzichten möchte, in Widerspruch geraten zu anderen Aussagen, für die dasselbe gilt. Über logische Manöver kann man dies Problem nicht lösen, sondern nur, wie in der Systemtherapie, mit Hilfe von Gegenparadoxierungen einen weniger schmerzhaften Ort suchen, an dem das Problem bis auf weiteres toleriert werden kann. Eben diese Einsicht führt aber zu dem Gedanken, daß die Paradoxieplacierung mehr oder weniger geschickt vorgenommen, mehr oder weniger deblockierend wirken, mehr oder weniger fruchtbar sein kann. Eine andere, nochmals verallgemeinerte Formulierung für diesen Sachverhalt wäre: daß der Schluß von Unbeschreibbarkeit auf Nichtexistenz logisch nicht begründet werden kann.

Wenn man mit Logik das Problem nur stellen, aber nicht lösen kann, liegt es nahe, sich nach anderen Möglichkeiten umzusehen. Die konstruktivistische Erkenntnistheorie sieht in Paradoxien, wie sollte sie anders, problematische Konstruktionen, die zu Umkonstruktionen des Wissens anregen. Die Theorie des Orientierungspluralismus sieht in Paradoxien ein gemeinsames Ausgangsproblem, das auf jeweils verschiedene Weise durch Unterscheidungen ("distinctions") ersetzt wird und damit den Anlaß gibt zum Aufbau unterschiedlicher Systeme kognitiver Komplexität, deren Sedimente uns schließlich als "Philosophie" erscheinen.[6] Die kybernetische Systemtheorie fragt, wie Systeme, die sich selbst beobachten können, die dabei auftretenden Paradoxien "invisibilisieren".[7] Klaus Krippendorff spricht nach einem Literaturüberblick über die informationstheoretische Behandlung von Paradoxien von einer Umwandlung unendlicher in endliche Informationslasten.[8] Ein Beobachter dieser Selbstbeobachtung mag dann erkennen, daß und wie diese Entparadoxierungen zu kreativen Ersatzlösungen führen. Die Lösungen, die dem sich reflektierenden System als natürlich und notwendig erscheinen, weil es anderenfalls eine der Gorgonen zu Gesicht bekäme, erscheinen dem Beobachter der Beobachter als artifiziell.[9] An die Stelle der für das System unsichtbaren, weil paradoxen, Einheit tritt die Rekursivität, die Führung der Operationen durch die Resultate der Operationen oder, auf der Ebene des Beobachtens, die Führung des Beobachtens durch die Resultate des Beobachtens. Im Ergebnis kommt dabei nicht eine logische Bereinigung der Weltprobleme heraus, sondern Aufbau kognitiver Komplexität - wozu immer.

Seit Kant zwischen dem Reich der Natur und dem Reich der Freiheit unterschied, um seine Antinomien aufzulösen, gilt das Unterscheiden als dasjenige Rezept, das hilft und das zu innovativer Wiederherstellung von Konsistenz sich eignet. Man muß nur auf die Unterscheidung kommen, die das Gewünschte leistet - empirisch/transzendental, Form und Substanz, Mehrheit von "Ebenen" der Analyse zum Beispiel. So weit so gut. Aber wie steht es dann mit den Paradoxien des Unterscheidens selbst, die zum Beispiel auftreten, wenn man an das Anfangen oder das Beenden des Unterscheidens denkt oder an universale Unterscheidungen (Weltbegriff, Sinnbegriff) oder an elementare, nicht weiter auflösbare Unterscheidungen? Danach fragt, im Anschluß an George Spencer Brown, Ranulph Glanville.[10]

Das Universalrezept des Unterscheidens universalisiert also nur das Problem. Der Erfolg des Rezepts "unterscheide!" macht nur deutlich, daß alles Erkennen letztlich im Unterscheiden besteht, also letztlich auf Paradoxien gegründet werden muß. Das gibt der Logik von George Spencer Brown ihre noch kaum erkannte Bedeutung für die Erkenntnistheorie, und im Anschluß daran entwickelt sich eine Terminologie, die Erkennen als Beobachten und Beschreiben versteht und Beobachten bzw. Beschreiben als Unterscheiden und Bezeichnen.

Ein Paradox ist ja immer ein Problem eines Beobachters. Wollte man behaupten, das Sein selbst wäre paradox, wäre eben diese Behauptung paradox. Paradoxien können deshalb nur behandelt werden, wenn man Beobachter beobachtet, und zwar aus einer Perspektive, die man heute Kybernetik zweiter Ordnung nennt. Jede Absicht auf vollständige Beschreibung, die nur Vollständigkeit erreichen kann, wenn sie sich selbst einbezieht, läuft auf dieses Problem auf. Stheno ist immer unter uns, und insofern haben die Recht (nur nicht: Erfolg), die sie auf dem Markt der postmodernen Diskurse zur Schau stellen wollen. Vielleicht läßt sich also das Problem auf eine Mehrheit von vernetzten Beobachtern verteilen. Jeder Beobachter beobachtet, was er beobachten kann, aufgrund seiner für ihn unsichtbaren Paradoxie, aufgrund einer Unterscheidung, deren Einheit sich seiner Beobachtung entzieht. Man hat die Wahl, ob man von wahr/unwahr, Krieg/Frieden, Frau/Mann, gut/böse, Heil/Verdammnis etc. ausgeht, aber wenn man für die eine oder die andere Unterscheidung optiert, hat man nicht mehr die Möglichkeit, die Unterscheidung als Einheit, als Form zu sehen - es sei denn mit Hilfe einer anderen Unterscheidung, also als ein anderer Beobachter. Auch die Anwendung einer solchen Unterscheidung auf sich selbst hilft nicht weiter. Im Gegenteil: sie endet im Paradox.

Jede Beobachtung braucht ihre Unterscheidung und also ihr Paradox der Identität des Differenten als ihren blinden Fleck, mit dessen Hilfe sie beobachten kann. Ein anderer Beobachter kann auch dies nur beobachten - aber nur bei anderen, nicht bei sich selber. Vielleicht liegt hier eine Möglichkeit, Latenzen und Einsichten zirkulieren zu lassen. Sthenographie braucht dann nicht unbedingt den Blick ins Paradox zu wagen und dann im postmodernen Erstarrungstanz sich selbst zu opfern. Es genügt, durchdachte Verfahren für das Beobachten von Beobachtungen zu entwickeln mit speziellem Interesse für das, was für den jeweils anderen paradox, also unbeobachtbar ist.

Wir hatten noch eine der grausigen Schwestern in Reserve gehalten. Vielleicht ist es Euryale, die solch einem Beobachter, der es geschickt vermeidet, sie zu beobachten, ihren Segen verleiht. Dann könnte man ein Interesse für kreative Entparadoxierung auch Euryalistik nennen.

II

Ein ganz ähnliches Problem verdanken wir dem Teufel, so wie der Teufel sich seinerseits diesem Problem verdankt. Ihn kann man allerdings sehen, oder jedenfalls riechen; und genau darin könnte ein Fortschritt liegen.

Wir wählen einen beliebig herausgegriffenen Text als Leitfaden: *"Non ebbe intenzione, a mio parere, Lucifero di farsi grande e rilevato per salire sopra Dio, perché in quel modo averebbe avuta intenzione non di sciogliere l'unità ma di miglioralia, il que poteva conoscere impossibile col solo dono naturale della scienza. Ebbe egli, dunque, pensiero d'inalzarsi col tirarsida un lato e partirsi dall uno formando il due, sopra del quale poscia, come sopra di centro, disegnò la sua circonferenza diversa quella di Dio; né si poteva partire dall'uno se non diventeva cattivo, perché tutto quelle che è buono, è uno. Iddio, tirando la linea dalla sua circonferenza, per formare il tre, creò l'uomo; il diavolo spinse anch'egli una linea dalla sua circonferenza per fare il quattro, e lo sedusse."*[11]

Der Text zeigt, nicht zufällig im Kontext der beginnenden modernen Staatstheorie, daß es nicht um Weltherrschaft geht, sondern um Beobachtung. Noch ist der Teufel nicht der Held schlechthin der Geschichte wie bei Milton oder Dryden. Erst recht ist es noch nicht der heutige Teufel, der Teufel des Superlativs und des "und dann?". Er ist nur getrieben durch den Impuls, das Eine, an dem er selbst teilhat, zu beobachten, und dadurch genötigt, eine Grenze zu ziehen, über die hinweg er beobachten kann (so wie der Privatopolitico, der Berater, der Fürst). Wenn aber das Eine das Gute ist (und wer darf am Fürstenhof das bezweifeln), wird der sich zur Beobachtung ausgrenzende Beobachter der Böse mit der Folge, daß dann nur noch ein Spiel des Sichabgrenzens möglich ist, dem sich der Mensch verdankt.

So wird verständlich, daß der Teufel als Vertreter einer Ordnung auftritt, die auf Unterscheidungen gebaut ist und diese festhalten muß. So tritt er im Mittelalter als Anwalt der Kosmologie einer allzu chaotisch wirkenden, Gott in Richtung Adhoc-kratie drängenden Maria entgegen.[12] So vertritt er - und selbst Marx, selbst Adorno werden ihm das noch verübeln - das Tauschprinzip, das Differenzen überwinden hilft, wenn auch nur mit Hilfe anderer Differenzen.[13] So erscheint er in würdevollem Ornat - als Großinquisitor. So wird er denn auch als "armer Teufel" gesehen; sei es (um die Furcht abzuschwächen) im Modus des Lächerlichen; sei es in melancholischer Gestalt als gefallener Engel, der die Schmutzarbeit des Seelenfangs verrichten muß, ohne recht zu wissen weshalb. Jedenfalls bleibt er ein sekundäres Prinzip - immer abhängig von dem, was man nicht ungestraft beobachten kann. Sein Problem ist die transzendentale Einheit des Einen, des Wahren und des Guten, die, wenn sie vorausgesetzt wird, den Beobachter des Beobachters dazu stimuliert, den, der die Einheit sehen will und sich deshalb gegen sie abgrenzen muß, als den Bösen zu beobachten und sich selbst daher als Sünder.

Während der christliche Teufel nur Gott beobachten will (und dies doch wohl durchaus im Sinne Gottes) und darüber zu Fall kommt, schafft Gott den Teufel des Islam unter dem Namen Iblis direkt durch eine paradoxe Weisung: verehre Adam! Iblis hält aber Gott für das einzig verehrungswürdige Wesen; er kann deshalb diese Weisung weder befolgen noch ablehnen. Er muß entscheiden und wird, so oder so, zum Bösen.[14] Derjenige, der das versucht, wird zu jemandem, der seinen Platz in der Ordnung der

Dinge nicht kennt, zu einem Ausbund an Klugheit und Torheit. Zugleich entsteht mit dem Versuch zur Auflösung der Paradoxie die Unterscheidung von gut und böse, die sich dann durch Religion programmieren läßt. Die noch klügeren Beobachter dieser paradoxen Beobachtung, die Theologen, können dann, zu spät allerdings, Tips geben, wie der Teufel seine Paradoxie besser hätte auflösen können; er hätte nämlich erkennen können, das Gott Adam die Seele eingegeben hat und daß er nur diese verehrt wissen wollte.

Gleichgültig, ob schon die Weisung paradox ist oder nur der Beobachtungsversuch selber: die Paradoxie macht es unmöglich, den Standort des Beobachters zu bestimmen. Er kann nur beobachten, daß er nicht beobachten kann. Aber in der alten Welt hatte alles, was ist, seinen Platz zu behalten. Ob Oktroi oder Versuch: die paradoxe Beobachtung sprengt diese Ordnung der festen Plätze. Sie kann dann interpretiert werden als Unzufriedenheit mit der gegebenen Placierung, als Absicht, über die eigene Stellung hinauszugelangen, als Übermut, Stolz, Neid, superbia, ambitio, curiositas - oder wie immer diese Sündentitel heißen. Und damit wird die Moral, die zu begründen wäre, vorausgesetzt und wiederhergestellt. Aber das ist nur möglich, solange man von der Einheit des Einen und des Guten ausgeht und damit das bezeichnet, wogegen der Teufel wie ein Untertan "rebelliert".[15]

Wir halten uns nicht mit den gesellschaftsstrukturellen Korrelaten und der Wissenssoziologie dieser Beobachtung transzendenter Einheit auf und versuchen auch keine immanente (z.B. logische oder differenztheoretische) Kritik. Wir bleiben beim Teufel. Einerseits wurde er mit Faust aufgewertet und zugleich abgewertet zum Gehilfen, wenn nicht zum Spott Fausts.[16] Andererseits hat ihn die biblische Hermeneutik der Beobachtbarkeit entzogen, indem sie ihm die (wissenschaftlich ausschlaggebende) Empirizität nahm und ihn auf eine Textexistenz reduzierte.[17] Es dürfte kein Zufall sein, daß zugleich auch der Beobachter mit dem neuen Titel "Subjekt" genötigt wurde, die Welt der Erfahrung zu fliehen. All dies sind jedoch Verlegenheitslösungen von einer bestenfalls transitorischen

Modernität. Man kann das übergehen und radikaler fragen: Was beobachtet ein Beobachter, der einen Beobachter beobachtet, der die Einheit, an der er selbst teilnimmt, zu beobachten versucht?

Ein solcher Beobachter *zweiter* Ordnung beobachtet eine *doppelte* Differenz. Er beobachtet zunächst einen Beobachter und beobachtet damit: *daß* dieser Beobachter beobachtet. Wie jede Operation zieht auch die Beobachtung eine Grenze um das, was sie tut. Sie unterscheidet *sich*. Außerdem aber hantiert sie *mit* einer Unterscheidung, um etwas unterscheiden und bezeichnen zu können. Oder genauer gesagt: sie ist eine Unterscheidung, die sich unterscheidet. Oder in der Terminologie von Bateson: sie produziert eine Information als "difference that makes a difference". Während der Beobachter erster Ordnung (und der Beobachter zweiter Ordnung ist in seiner Operation immer auch ein Beobachter erster Ordnung) die Unterscheidung, die er seiner Beobachtung zugrundelegt, nur anwendet, macht der Beobachter zweiter Ordnung diese Unterscheidung zum Gegenstand einer weiteren Unterscheidung. Er beobachtet diesen Beobachter - und nichts anderes. Und er beobachtet, *wie* der Beobachter beobachtet, das heißt: mit welcher Unterscheidung - ob als Moralist oder als Physiker, ob als Philosoph im Hinblick auf das Wesen der Dinge oder als König im Hinblick auf Ruhe oder Unruhe der Untertanen.

Der Schritt von der Beobachtung erster zur Beobachtung zweiter Ordnung löst eine ganze Kaskade von Folgen aus. Nur eines erreicht er nicht: die Beobachtung der ihn selbst einschließenden Einheit, die Rückkehr in den "unmarked space". Die Beobachtung zweiter Ordnung ersetzt die Einheit durch die doppelte Differenz. Sie kann auf diese Weise zur Selbstbeobachtung werden, wenn sie ein System bildet, in dem beobachtet werden kann, wie im System beobachtet wird. Das kann zu Bewußtseinstheorien oder zu Gesellschaftstheorien führen je nach der Systemreferenz, die der Selbstbeobachtung zugrundeliegt. Aber auch die Selbstbeobachtung vollzieht eine Differenz und grenzt, indem sie intern Anschlußfähigkeit sucht, anderes aus. Jede weitere Reflexion des Beobachtens führt auf die mit dem Beobachten erzeugte Differenz zurück - auch dann, wenn man die Unterscheidungen auswechselt, mit denen die Beobachtungen arbeiten, also zum Beispiel die Moralisten psychologisch oder soziologisch entlarvt als in Wahrheit durch Triebdifferenzen oder durch Klassendifferenzen motiviert. Es bleibt die Möglichkeit, intern bestimmte Beobachtungen als "Repräsentation" oder als "Zeichen" oder als "Symbol" auszuzeichnen, ihnen also eine Funktion für die Bezeichnung der Einheit der Differenz von System und Umwelt zuzusprechen. Aber gerade dies ist nun um so mehr eine interne Bezeichnung aufgrund einer intern relevanten Unterscheidung, die intern dem Beobachten zugrunde gelegt wird und intern ausgewechselt werden könnte. So spricht die Reflexionstheorie, und ihre Symbolik ist unweigerlich diabolisch angelegt, weil Einheit nur mit Hilfe von Unterscheidungen zu beobachten und eine Beobachtung nur als Vollzug einer Differenz zu vollziehen ist.

Die symbolisch-diabolische Einheit des Beobachtens der Einheit, die das Beobachten einschließt (und "einschließt" immer in dem Sinne, daß anderes dadurch ausgeschlossen wird), zeigt sich dem Beobachter zweiter Ordnung als Paradoxie eines solchen Versuchs. Darin liegt nicht zuletzt eine Paradoxie der Zeit. Die Gorgonen hatten auf Lähmung gesetzt. Dem Teufel sind dynamische Perspektiven zu danken. Ihm bleibt aber seine nicht kurierbare Obsession mit Moral vorzuwerfen. Mit heutigen Theoriemitteln kann man davon (ohne Verlust an Rekonstruktionsfähigkeit) abstrahieren. Die Paradoxie läßt den Beobachter oszillieren, nämlich ganz kurzzeitig (aber immerhin: kurzzeitig) zwischen der einen Feststellung und ihrem Gegenteil pendeln. Wenn man aber die Position eines Beobachters zweiter Ordnung einnimmt, kann man zugleich beobachten, wie der Beobachter erster Ordnung sich verhält, wie er sich seine Paradoxie invisibilisiert, wie er sie durch Unterscheidungen ersetzt und verstellt, wie er unbestimmbare in bestimmbare Komplexität umwandelt und damit zu endlichen Informationslasten kommt. Der Beobachter zweiter Ordnung ist dann keineswegs gehalten, es ebenso zu machen. Aber er kann wenigstens sehen, daß es möglich ist, und vielleicht ist er Funktionalist genug, um nach anderen, funktional äquivalenten Lösungen für das Problem Ausschau zu halten.

III

Sieht man das Fundierungsparadox als Problem, das mit jeglicher Unterscheidung mitgegeben ist, kann man darin zugleich ein Bezugsproblem für funktionale Analysen ausmachen und fragen, welche funktional äquivalenten Möglichkeiten der Auflösung des Paradoxes erkennbar sind. Paradoxien sind unvermeidlich, sobald die Welt (der "unmarked space" Spencer Browns) durch irgendeine Unterscheidung verletzt wird. Das feiert, wie immer pervers, die Sthenographie. Eine Euryalistik könnte sich darum kümmern, welche Unterscheidungen welche Paradoxien erzeugen und mit welchen Theorieleistungen das Problem dann an der Unterscheidung kuriert werden kann. Und die Vermutung ist, daß es hierfür verschiedene, mehr oder weniger fruchtbare, funktional äquivalente Möglichkeiten gibt - je nachdem, mit welcher Unterscheidung man die Paradoxie konstruiert und auflöst.[18] Wir wollen, als eine Art Eignungsbeweis für Systemtheorie, zeigen, wie dies geschehen kann, wenn man von der Unterscheidung System und Umwelt ausgeht.

Zerteilt man die Welt durch die Unterscheidung von System und Umwelt, so entstehen bestimmte Folgeprobleme. Gleichgültig, welches System man meint und was demzufolge Umwelt ist: es lassen sich nicht mehr alle Phänomene verorten. Die Unterscheidung postuliert zwar Weltrelevanz (Universalität), denn für sie ist alles entweder System oder Umwelt; aber zugleich lassen sich die die Unterscheidung konstituierenden Momente selbst nicht in dieser Unterscheidung verorten. Die Einheit des Systems findet man weder im System noch in der Umwelt, und auch die Grenzen des Systems findet man weder im System noch in der Umwelt. Der übliche Ausweg ist: einen Beobachter zu postulieren, der bezeichnet, was *für ihn* (in *seiner* Umwelt) das System und dessen Grenzen sind. Dieser Beobachter läßt sich aber nicht als Subjekt und auch nicht extramundan ansetzen, denn das würde einen weiteren Beobachter mit entsprechend potenzierten Eigenschaften, also ein Subsubjekt erfordern. In der Welt kann der Beobachter aber wiederum nur ein System sein (denn sonst verliert die Ausgangsunterscheidung ihre Universalität), und dann hat man die Frage, wie denn dieses System die konstituierenden Momente seiner Unterscheidung in seiner Welt unterbringt.

An die Stelle der traditionellen Lösung, die eine Externalisierung des Beobachters erforderte und im extramundanen Subjekt ihren letzten idealen Stützpunkt postulieren mußte, muß die Systemtheorie deshalb eine andere Lösung setzen. Das kann geschehen, wenn man annimmt, daß die Unterscheidung von System und Umwelt jeweils von einem System getroffen wird und daher mit all ihren Folgen eine systemeigene Leistung ist und bleibt. Die Umwelt kann nicht unterscheiden. Sie kann überhaupt nicht operieren. Ein System kann in seiner Umwelt andere Systeme beobachten, denen es Operationen und Unterscheidungen zurechnen kann; aber das sind dann Systeme in der Umwelt desjenigen Systems, das sich zunächst von seiner Umwelt unterschieden hat. Entsprechend ist alle Grenzziehung immer Grenzziehung eines Systems. Die Umwelt zieht keine Grenzen um das System. Das System grenzt sich selbst aus, und die Umwelt kann das weder registrieren noch beobachten, weder wissen noch irgendwie anders nachvollziehen. Die Grenzen haben nur von innen gesehen Form, nur von innen gesehen eine Innenseite und eine Außenseite. Und das liegt ja eigentlich auf der Hand: man kann die Außenseite der Systemgrenze nicht gut als ihre Innenseite von seiten der Umwelt ansehen.

Das Gleiche gilt für die Einheit des Systems. Sie ist Einheit aufgrund der im System selbst produzierten Anschlußfähigkeit der systemeigenen Operationen. Sie ist das, was sich ergibt, wenn das System rekursiv operiert. Für die Umwelt existiert diese Einheit nicht, da die Umwelt sie weder unterscheiden noch bezeichnen könnte. Und wieder: es mag Systeme in der Umwelt geben, die Dank eigener Operations- und Unterscheidungsfähigkeit die Einheit des System, von dem wir ausgehen, bezeichnen können. Aber wenn man wissen will, wie dies geschieht, muß man diejenigen Systeme beobachten, die jeweils als Beobachter fungieren – und das sind Systeme in der Umwelt des Systems, das sich auf diese Weise beobachtet wissen kann.

Mit Hilfe der Logik von George Spencer Brown kann man diesen Sachverhalt auch als Wiedereintritt derUnterscheidung (von System und Umwelt) in das durch sie Unterschiedene (in das System) beschreiben. Wenn wir in diesem Text diesen Wiedereintritt beschreiben, erscheint er uns als Paradoxie; denn er postuliert, daß die Ausgangsunterscheidung dieselbe und nicht dieselbe ist, wie die, die in sie wieder eintritt. Das beobachtete System dagegen behandelt die Unterscheidung von System und Umwelt als eine interne Kopplung von Selbstreferenz und Fremdreferenz, an der es alle eigenen Operationen orientiert, um sie als eigene beobachten und vollziehen zu können. Und es braucht nicht zu berücksichtigen (und kann es einem Beobachter zweiter Ordnung überlassen festzustellen), daß eben dadurch, daß dies geschieht, die Differenz von System und Umwelt überhaupt erst erzeugt wird.

Man kann diese Linien weiter ausziehen und stößt dann auf bereits bekannte Theoriekomplexe - etwa auf die Theorie selbstreferentieller autopoietischer Systeme, auf die Kybernetik zweiter Ordnung (die Kybernetik beobachtender Systeme) oder auf die konstruktivistische Erkenntnistheorie. Die Systemtheorie, die sich der Unterscheidung von System und Umwelt bedient, um ihre eigene Paradoxie zu finden und aufzulösen, erzeugt für sich selber das, was sie als Konstitutionsmerkmal von Systemen postuliert, nämlich Anschlußfähigkeit. Nicht so offensichtlich ist, daß mit der Ausführung dieses Forschungsprogramms hochgetriebene Genauigkeitsansprüche verbunden sind, die man zunächst nicht erwarten würde, wenn man die Selbstfundierung der Theorie in einer Paradoxie und die durchgehende Verwendung von Zirkeln als Gegenstandsmerkmal und als Argumentationsfigur bedenkt. So muß vor allem das, was als autopoietische Operation bezeichnet wird, in einer Weise präzise bestimmt werden, die jede "anthropologische" Fundierung ausschließt, die sich mit Unterscheidungen wie Mensch/Tier oder Mensch/Gott begnügen muß oder heute vorzugsweise selbst das noch im Unklaren läßt, wovon sie den Menschen unterscheidet. Jeder weitere Schritt in Richtung auf eine präzise Bestimmung der selbstreferentiellen Operation, deren rekursive Vernetzung das System ausdifferenziert, muß infolgedessen genau überlegt werden. Das zwingt vermutlich (1) zur Festlegung auf "Ereignisse" als basale Elemente anstelle von zeitfest bestehenden Einheiten wie Atomen, Zellen, Menschen, Sternen etc. und (2) zur Unterscheidung unterschiedlicher Operationsweisen (Ereignisverknüpfungen), namentlich zur strikten Trennung von bewußten und kommunikativen Operationen.[19] Auch wenn sich in diesen Hinsichten andere Optionen entwickeln und als überlegen erweisen sollten und auch wenn ganz andere Ausgangsunterscheidungen, etwa die von Form und Medium oder die von Reden und Schweigen als funktional äquivalent ausprobiert werden können: die Anregung, Unterscheidungen zur Konstruktion und Auflösung von Paradoxien (also paradox) zu verwenden, läuft auf Anforderungen an Theoriebildung hinaus, die nicht so leicht zu befriedigen sind. Die Systemtheorie kann das heute schon modellhaft vorführen.

IV

Und nun kann man sehen: alles Begründen verwickelt sich in eine Paradoxie. Wenn man die Suche nach Gründen als Tätigkeit beobachtet, erscheint sie als eine paradoxe Operation. Jedes Begründen setzt sich durch den bloßen Vollzug (und auch durch den Vollzug einer Frage oder einer unendlichen Suche) dem Vergleich mit anderen Möglichkeiten und damit dem Selbstzweifel aus. Die Begründung produziert auf der Suche nach Notwendigem Kontingenzen. Sie operiert kontraintuitiv. Sie entfernt sich von dem Ziel, das sie anstrebt. Sie sabotiert sich laufend selbst, indem sie einen Zugang zu anderen Möglichkeiten eröffnet, wo sie ihn verschliessen möchte. Geschlossenheit ist nur mit Hilfe einer Differenz erreichbar, nur als Eingeschlossensein in den Zusammenhang der eigenen Rekursivität, nur als Systembildung. Die Erzeugung von Geschlossenheit ist der operative Vollzug der Erzeugung von Geschlossenheit, und nicht etwas, was man als Grund vorfinden könnte, von dem man ausgehen oder den man entdecken kann. Der Grund kann nur in der Tätigkeit des Begründens liegen, in den künstlichen Redundanzen, die sie aufbaut, also in der funktionierenden Rekursivität des Begründens, also in dem System, das sie bildet.

Vielleicht haben Theologen das immer schon gewußt, wenn sie es für nötig hielten, sich von Weltsachen zu distanzieren. Wir bemerken das als Beobachter. Und auch die Systemtheorie kann als Grund nur die Autopoiesis der Systeme nennen, die Autonomie des faktischen Vollzugs der Selbstproduktion als Einschließung in die Welt. Wir bemerken das als Beobachter.

V

Schließlich noch eine Bemerkung zur systemischen Therapie und der ins Praktische gewendeten Sthenographie. Dies ist, vordergründig betrachtet, ein moderner Fall von Teufelsaustreibung. Paradox gegen Paradox, Konstruktion gegen Konstruktion und die Hilfe muß aus Dir selbst kommen, denn Du bist ein System. Auch hier ist es dann aber nützlich, vom Teufel auf die Gorgonen zurückzugehen. Es geht darum, Grausen einzujagen und zugleich zu lehren, das Paradox zu beobachten und nicht zu beobachten. Der Therapeut verbirgt sich hinter seiner "Weisung", seiner Stheno, seinem contraparadosso. Er tritt gorgonisch maskiert auf. Um Hilfe gerufen, lehrt er: Dein Problem ist schlimm, behalte es; es ist für Dich notwendig, ist Dir lieb, ist Dir teuer (bis hin zur Bereitschaft, den zu bezahlen, der Dir das sagt).

Die Soziologie hat dieser Therapieform bisher wenig Beachtung geschenkt. Würde sie es tun, würde sie sich selbst wiedererkennen. Ob nun in den milderen Formen des Marxismus oder in den schärferen der Systemtheorie: der Soziologe sieht, wie Kynéas, über den Superlativ hinaus: neu, neuer, am neuesten, am allerneuesten - und dann? Er durchschaut den Strukturschutz der Latenzen der

Gesellschaft. Er sieht mit den Kybernetikern zweiter Ordnung, daß die Gesellschaft nicht sieht, daß sie nicht sieht, was sie nicht sieht. Er sagt es und wünscht, sich verabschiedend, der Gesellschaft eine neue Zukunft.

Immerhin ist es eine Eigenart dieser Beschreibung, daß sie, nicht nur als Praxis, sondern auch als Theorie, für sich selbst transparent ist. In ihrer Selbstbeobachtung verwendet sie ihrerseits eine Unterscheidung. Aber welche? Für Kynéas war die Sache klar: Nachdem Italien, Spanien, der Orient, ja der ganze Weltkreis erobert sei, wolle man sich zu einem Trinkgelage niederlassen und sich ausruhen?[20] Aber wenn das der Eigenwert ist: warum nicht gleich so? Wer sich vom Teufel versucht sah, konnte auf Gnade hoffen. Aber welchen Gegenbegriff erfordert die Sthenographie? In der alten Welt der Gorgonen sicher den Begriff der Stadt (später dann: den des Gartens), wo man sich sicher fühlen kann. Das verweist auf eine Zentrum/Peripherie-Differenzierung der Gesellschaft. In der heutigen Weltgesellschaft ist diese Unterscheidung nichtmehr anwendbar oder allenfalls noch für die politischen Schönheitsfarmen der Grünen geeignet. Aber was tritt an ihre Stelle?

Die Systemtherapie würde ihr eigenes Reflexionsdefizit offenlegen, wenn sie diese Frage nicht stellen würde. Sie stellen heißt aber noch nicht: sie beantworten. Wir haben Sthenographie und Euryalistik unterschieden, aber der zweite Begriff markiert nur den Raum, an dem die Antwort sich zeigen, und vermutlich: erschreckend zeigen sollte. So wie die Analyse hier angelegt ist (aber: andere Unterscheidungen, andere Phänomene, sagen wir), kann nur eine differenztheoretisch angesetzte Fragetechnik weiterführen. Das liefe auf ein Ausprobieren von universell praktizierbaren Unterscheidungen hinaus, die einerseits logisch reflexiv gebaut sein müßten, das heißt eine Form bieten müßten, die in sich selbst wiedereingeführt werden kann; und andererseits wechselseitig aufeinander beziehbar sein müßten, so daß sich ein rekursives Netzwerk von Operationen bilden läßt, in dem Anschlußfähigkeit garantiert ist. Weder Logik noch Erkenntnistheorie könnten dann einen sicheren Ausgangspunkt bilden, da beide die für sie maßgebenden Unterscheidungen bereits unter besonderen Konditionen praktizieren, die die Besonderheit von Logik bzw. Erkenntnistheorie im Unterschied zu anderen Operationsweisen definieren. Aber es gibt inzwischen genug Angebote, die den oben skizzierten Bedingungen genügen. System und Umwelt ist nur eines von ihnen, Differenz und Identität ein weiteres, Operation und Beobachtung ein drittes, Form und Medium ein viertes. Es wird für den Theoriestil sicher einen Unterschied ausmachen, mit welcher Unterscheidung man eine Praxis des operativen Kondensierens und Differenzierens anfängt. Das heißt auch, daß es sich immer um in der Willkür des Anfangs und der eigenen Geschichte begründete Theorie handeln wird.[21] Und das wiederum heißt (wenn man "Willkür" als Signal nimmt für die Weisung: Beobachte den Beobachter), daß solche Theorieentwicklungen im Bereich dessen bleiben, was sich der Beobachtung aussetzt. Als Soziologe wird man der Meinung sein, daß dies letztlich auf Gesellschaft (und damit auf ein System in einer Umwelt) verweist als Bedingung der Möglichkeit des Beobachtens von Beobachtungen. Aber ein Künstler zum Beispiel könnte es anders sehen.

Anmerkungen

[1] MacKie, J. L., 1973, *Truth, Probability and the Paradox: Studies in Philosophical Logic*. Oxford, S. 239.
[2] Vgl. außer MacKie, a.a.O. auch Chihara, C. S., 1973, *Ontology and the Vicious Circle Principle*. Ithaca.
[3] Siehe dazu Atlan, H., 1986, *A tort et à raison: Intercritique de la science et du mythe*. Paris, S. 73 f. zu: L'auto-référence du langage et les blancs de l'écriture.
[4] *Reflexivity: The Post-Modern Predicament*. London 1985.
[5] Genau an dieser Stelle setzt die Logik von George Spencer Brown an - nur um dann ihrerseits Paradoxien der Form zu erzeugen. Siehe Brown, G.S., 1971, *Laws of Form* 2. Aufl. London, und dazu Glanville, R./Varela, F., "Your Inside is Out and Your Outside is In (Beatles 1968)", in: Lasker, G.E., Hg., 1981 *Applied Systems and Cybernetics*. Bd. II, New York, S. 638-641.
[6] So Rescher, N., 1985, *The Strife of Systems: An Essay on the Grounds and Implications of Philosophical Diversity*. Pittsburgh 1985.

7 So Barel, Y., 1983, "De la fermeture à l'ouverture en passant par l'autonomie?" In: Dumouchel, P./Dupuy, J.P., Hgg., *L'auto-organisation: De la physique au politique*. Paris, S. 466-475. Vgl. auch ders., 1979, *Le paradoxe et le système: Essai sur le fantastique social*. Grenoble.

8 Siehe: Paradox and Information, in: Dervin. B./Voigt, M.J., Hgg., 1984, *Progress in Communication Sciences* Bd. 5, Norwood, N.J., S. 45-71.

9 Diese Unterscheidung macht Löfgren, L., 1978, "Some Foundational Views on General Systems and the Hempel Paradox". In: *International Journal of General Systems 4* , S. 243-253.

10 Vgl. oben Anm. 7. Siehe auch Glanville, R., 1984, "Distinguished and Exact Lies". In: Trappl, R., Hg., *Cybernetics and Systems Research 2*. Amsterdam, S. 655-662.

11 Malvezzi, V., *Ritratto del Privato politico christiano*. Zit. nach Opere del Marchese Malvezzi 1635, Mediolanum, S. 235 f.

12 Vgl. Spangenberg, P.-M., 1987, *Maria ist immer und überall: Die Alltagswelten des spätmittelalterlichen Mirakels* Frankfurt, passim, insb. S. 233 f. Auch spätere Zeiten werden diese Tradition noch bewahren und Erlösung als Erlösung vom Recht begreifen, als "delivering us from ... the Severity, Justice and Curse of the Law", wie es bei Reynolds, E., 1640, *A Treatise of the Passions and Faculties of the Soule of Man*. London, Nachdruck Gainesville, Fla. 1971, S. 422 heißt.

13 Der Stein des Anstoßes war, wie bekannt: die Ausdehnung des Prinzips auf etwas Unvertauschbares, auf die Seele! Aber dann: wer beobachtet *diese* Differenz und wer die Paradoxie des Vertauschens von Unvertauschbarem?

14 Vgl. Schimmel, A., 1975, *Mystical Dimensions of Islam*. Chapel Hill, N.C., S. 193ff.

15 Wir erlauben uns die Nebenbemerkung, daß sein Rang, sein Adel unbestritten ist und unter Theologen und Angelologen allenfalls noch über seine Placierung in der Hierarchie diskutiert wird.

16 So weit treibt es Valéry, P., *Mon Faust*, zit. nach Œuvres. 1960, Bd. 2, Paris, S. 276-403.

17 So Mayer, J.G., 1780, *Historia diaboli, seu commentatio de diaboli malorumque spirituum existentia, statibus, judiciis, consiliis postestate*. 2. Aufl., Tübingen. Dies wird nochmals überboten durch eine heute vertretene Auffassung: das, was der Teufel sei, könne nur der Begriffsgeschichte entnommen werden. So Russell, J.B., 1984, *Lucifer: The Devil in the Middle Ages*. Ithaca, N.Y., insb. S. 22 ff.

18 "Konstruiert *und* auflöst" - man beachte *diese* Paradoxie!

19 Tendenziell ähnlich, aber nicht in einem systemtheoretischen sondern in einem linguistischen Theoriezusammenhang Lyotard, J.-F., 1983, *Le différend*. Paris. Die Operation heißt hier "phrase". Sie ist als Ereignis konzipiert. Sie kommt durch rekursive Verknüpfung mit anderen Ereignissen gleicher Art zustande (enchaînement) und erzeugt durch Bedingungen dieser Verknüpfung (genres de discours, régimes de phrases) Ausgrenzungen, die einen "différend" mitproduzieren, den zu vermeiden es keine Möglichkeit gibt, wenn man "phrase" als Operation verwendet. Jeder Metadiskurs würde nur für sich selbst diesen Effekt reproduzieren.

20 Plutarch, Pyrrhus XIV. In einer der frühesten "bürgerlichen" (politökonomischen) Theorien der Neuzeit wurde übrigens genau diese Geschichte des thessalischen Redners am Hofe des Königs Pyrrhos aufgegriffen, aber in der Bestimmung des Letztwertes von privatem Genuß auf nationale ökonomische Prosperität (gegen den Militarismus des Adels) umstilisiert. Siehe Crucé, E., 1623, *Le nouveau Cynée ou Discours d'Estat*. Zit. nach der Neuausgabe mit engl. Übersetzung von Balch, T.W., 1909, Philadelphia.

21 Ich nenne in der Aufzählung die jeweils re-entry-fähige Seite der Unterscheidung zuerst.

Hinweise zu den Autoren

Niklas *Luhmann*, geb. 1927 in Lüneburg. Nach dem Studium der Rechtswissenschaft und nach mehrjähriger Tätigkeit in der Öffentlichen Verwaltung 1966 Promotion und Habilitation an der Universität Münster. Seit 1968 Professor für Soziologie an der Fakultät für Soziologie der Universität Bielefeld. Neuere Publikationen: Gesellschaftsstruktur Semantik, 2 Bde. (1980/81), Liebe als Passion (1982), Soziale Systeme (1984), Ökologische Kommunikation (1986), Die Wirtschaft der Gesellschaft (1988).

Humberto R. *Maturana*, geb. 1928, ist Neurobiologe und arbeitet an der Universidad de Santiago/Chile. Er promovierte an der Harvard University im Fach Biologie, studierte anschließend Medizin in Santiago und war dann Mitarbeiter verschiedener Forschungsprojekte in den USA und in England. Auf deutsch sind grundlegende Arbeiten Maturanas veröffentlicht in dem Sammelband 'Erkennen: Die Organisation und Verkörperung von Wirklichkeit', (1982); 1987 erschien das gemeinsam mit seinem ehemaligen Schüler Francisco Varela geschriebene Buch 'Der Baum der Erkenntnis. Die biologischen Wurzeln des menschlichen Erkennens'.

Mikio *Namiki*, geb. 1925 in Tokio/Japan, promovierte 1953 an der School of Science and Engineering der Waseda University in Tokio, habilitierte 1960 an der Tokyo University of Science and Literature und ist seit 1965 Professor für Physik an der Waseda University. Einige Publikationen (auf Japanisch): Quantum Mechanics I, II (1978), Delta Function and Differential Equations (1982), Uncertainty Principle (1982).

Francisco J. *Varela*, geb. 1946 in Chile, studierte Medizin und Naturwissenschaften an der Universidad de Chile in Santiago. Promotion zum Dr. phil. in Biologie 1970 an der Harvard University. Seither Lehrtätigkeit und Forschung an den Universitäten von Chile, Costa Rica und den medizinischen Fakultäten der Universitäten von Colorado und von New York.

Derzeit an der Ecole Polytechnique in Paris. Autor von über vierzig Forschungsberichten über neurobiologische, mathematisch-kybernetische und wissenschaftstheoretische Fragen. Weitere Publikationen u.a.: Principles of Biological Autonomy und (zusammen mit Humberto Maturana, 1987) Der Baum der Erkenntnis.

Volker *Redder* ist Kollegiat am Siegener Graduiertenkolleg.

Materialität der Zeichen

Reihe A

Bisher erschienen:

Gisela Smolka-Koerdt/
Peter M. Spangenberg/
Dagmar Tillmann-Bartylla, Hrsg.
Der Ursprung von Literatur
Medien, Rollen, Kommunikationssituationen zwischen 1450 und 1650
304 S. Geb. 3-7705-2461-6

Wolfgang Scherer
Klavier-Spiele
Die Psychotechnik der Klaviere im 18. und 19. Jahrhundert
237 S. Geb. 3-7705-2580-9

Niklas Luhmann/
Umberto Manturana/
Mikio Namiki/
Volker Redder/Francisco Varela
Beobachter
Konvergenz der Erkenntnistheorien?
140 S. Geb. 3-7705-2526-4

K. Ludwig Pfeiffer/Michael Walter
Kommunikationsformen als Lebensformen
309 S. Geb. 3-7705-2658-9

Bernhard J. Dotzler
Der Hochstapler
Thomas Mann und die Simulakren der Literatur
156 S. Geb. 3-7705-2682-1

Ulrike Dünkelsbühler
Kritik der Rahmen-Vernunft
Parergon-Versionen nach Kant und Derrida
187 S. Geb. 3-7705-2683-X

Bernhard J. Dotzler
Technopathologien
295 S. Kart. 3-7705-2726-7

Benno Wagner
Im Dickicht der politischen Kultur
Parlamentarismus, Alternativen und Mediensymbolik vom „Deutschen Herbst" bis zur „Wende"
366 S. Geb. 3-7705-2715-1

Friedrich Balke/Eric Méchoulan/
Benno Wagner
Zeit des Ereignisses – Ende der Geschichte?
325 S. Kart. 3-7705-2527-2

Michael Walter (Hrsg.)
Text und Musik
Neue Perspektiven der Theorie
253 S. Kart. 3-7705-2758-5

Wilhelm Fink Verlag · München